INSPIRED BY A TRUE STORY

SUSAN APPEL

LUCIDBOOKS

What the Heart Carries
One Secret, Two Lives

Published by Lucid Books in Houston, TX
www.LucidBooks.com

eISBN: 978-1-63296-969-9
Paperback ISBN: 978-1-63296-967-5
Hardback ISBN: 978-1-63296-968-2

Special Sales: Most Lucid Books titles are available in special quantity discounts. Custom imprinting or excerpting can also be done to fit special needs. Contact Lucid Books at Info@LucidBooks.com.

Editorial Services: Erika's Editing

To my brother

Table of Contents

For all that is secret will eventually be brought into the open, and everything that is concealed will be brought to light and made known to all.

—Luke 8:17

CHAPTER 1: THE BEGINNING (1966)

Cecilia adjusted the strap of her purse as she walked along 86th Street under the El, the scent of fresh Italian bread and coffee drifting from the corner bakery. Car horns, laughter, and the distant rumble of the subway filled the air, but her mind was focused on the errand her mother had sent her on. She was to pick up a spool of thread from the fabric store and then head straight home. Simple. Routine.

Just as she arrived at the corner of Stillwell Avenue, she stopped short at the sight of him. Through the large glass window of the neighborhood gym, she saw a man, his dark hair slicked back, his muscular arms flexing as he lifted a pair of weights. Stunned, her breath caught in her throat. He was unlike any man she'd ever seen before—confident, strong, and completely engrossed in his workout. A few girls near the gym's entrance were watching him as well. Giggling, they stole glances in the man's direction. They were animated and giddy, but Cecilia was rooted in place, unable to move, unable to look away.

Then, as if sensing her gaze, he turned. Their eyes met through the glass.

Cecilia's heart thudded in her chest. For a moment she considered looking away and pretending she hadn't been staring, but something about the man's expression—the amused smirk, the spark of curiosity in his eyes—held her there. Slowly, deliberately, he set the weights down and wiped the sweat from his brow. Then, to her surprise, he walked over to the door.

Cecilia panicked. She knew she should leave, turn on her heels and pretend this never happened. But before she could make herself move, he was walking straight toward her.

"Enjoying the view?" he asked as he approached, his voice deep and playful.

She felt herself blush. "I was just passing by."

His smirk widened. "Sure you were."

She folded her arms, trying to steady herself. "Well, are you going to tell me your name?"

"James," he said, offering his hand. "And you?"

"Cecilia. Cecilia Russo."

Their hands met, and an undeniable current passed between them. Cecilia swallowed hard. She had heard about men like him—charmers, flirts, troublemakers—the kind of men her mother had warned her about.

And yet as he held her gaze, none of that mattered. Awestruck, Cecilia could only think about this man named James.

"I've never seen you around here before," James said, tilting his head slightly. "Are you new to the neighborhood?"

She shook her head. "No. I live a few blocks away. My mother sent me to the fabric store."

James grinned. "Exciting afternoon, then."

She laughed despite herself. "Not quite as exciting as lifting weights in front of an audience."

He chuckled, stepping a little closer. "I don't mind an audience, especially when it includes a girl as pretty as you."

At the compliment, Cecilia fought again the urge to blush. She should have walked away. She should have smiled politely, excused herself, and continued on her errand. Instead, she lingered, drawn in by the easy confidence in his voice and the way his eyes darkened when they met hers.

"I should go," she murmured, though she made no move to leave.

James studied her for a moment and then cocked his chin just a bit. "Alright. But let me walk you to the store."

She hesitated, knowing she should refuse. But despite her better judgment, she found herself nodding. And so they walked side by side, the summer sun casting long shadows on the sidewalk as they went.

That evening, as Cecilia and her family sat down to dinner, her sister Linda quietly scolded her: "You shouldn't talk to men like that."

Their mother, Concetta, bustled around the kitchen scooping out steaming portions of pasta, oblivious to the conversation between the twins.

"Daddy would've had a fit if he'd seen you flirting this afternoon with that guy outside the gym," Linda continued.

Cecilia rolled her eyes but kept her voice low. "I wasn't flirting."

Linda snorted. "Please. You didn't realize it, but I was by Mr. Morelli's soda shop a few doors down. I saw the way that man looked at you—and the way you looked at him."

Their father, Leo, sat at the head of the table. He was a man of principle, his presence alone commanding respect. He was unaware of the tension building between the twins. The girls were always whispering, and he took no notice of it.

Cecilia had spent her life trying to be the good daughter, the obedient one. But this evening, for the first time, she felt a pull toward something—someone—that didn't fit neatly into her world.

Cecilia's family was loving but strict. Her father was a retired boxer and former Navy man, and he ran their household with a firm but caring hand. He had worked tirelessly to provide for his family, instilling discipline and respect in his children. Their home was warm and filled with the aromas of baked ziti, sautéed broccoli rabe, and chicken parmesan, but there were many unspoken rules. Cecilia knew those rules well, and today she had broken one of them for the first time.

Then there was James and Cecilia's first real date. It was anything but ordinary. James pulled up to the corner of her block—out of sight of Cecilia's parents—in a sleek, black 1965 Pontiac GTO, its polished chrome gleaming under the streetlights. The low rumble of the engine sent a thrill through Cecilia as she slipped into the passenger seat.

She had told her parents she was going to the movies with Linda, which wasn't a complete lie—Linda was coming along. But their parents didn't know anything about James or their real plans for the evening, and her parents certainly didn't know that James was bringing along his friend Tony as a date for Linda.

Linda sat in the back seat, exchanging flirtatious glances with Tony. Cecilia could hardly focus on anything but James's hand resting casually on the gear shift. He drove with an effortless cool, weaving through the streets of Brooklyn in the evening light.

As they reached Coney Island, the scent of salt water and fried food was thick in the air. The two couples walked along the boardwalk, the sounds of carnival rides and laughter surrounding them. James bought Cecilia some cotton candy, his fingers grazing hers as he handed it over. The touch sent a shiver through her. They wandered through the games where James easily won her a stuffed bear. When they rode the Wonder Wheel, he rocked their seat just enough to make her laugh and grip his arm.

As the night stretched on, Cecilia felt the weight of the rules she was breaking, but with James beside her, it didn't seem to matter. The way he looked at her, like she was the only girl in the world, made her forget everything else.

When they pulled up to a spot just a few doors down from her house, Cecilia noticed that the porch light was on—a reminder of the world she had to return to. James leaned over, brushing his hand against her cheek. "I had a good time tonight," he said.

She beamed with delight, her heart pounding. "Me too."

For a moment, it seemed like he might kiss her, but instead, James simply grinned.

"Sweet dreams, Cecilia."

The weeks flew by, and Cecilia never told her parents about her new boyfriend. She swore Linda to secrecy. Her twin often covered for her. As Cecilia got to know James better, their stolen meetings became more frequent, and their conversations got deeper.

It wasn't long before one night, parked at a secluded spot near the Verrazzano Bridge, James kissed Cecilia with an urgency she had never known before. The city lights shimmered in the distance as his hands traced her skin, each touch setting fire to her senses. She knew nice girls didn't do this, that she was breaking both her parents' rules and God's. Yet she gave herself to him completely, believing in the moment, believing in him.

∞ ∞ ∞

Fatigue. It washed over her whole body, a tired ache she'd never felt before. At first she thought it was the flu, but then the nausea started. One morning as she leaned over the toilet bowl, the realization hit her like a tidal wave: She was pregnant.

But the real devastation came when Junior, her older brother, spotted her and James together one afternoon. When they parted, Junior followed James to an old brownstone. There, Junior saw James slip his wedding ring on at the top of the stairs before unlocking the door.

Cecilia could barely breathe as Junior told their father. The house erupted into chaos, her mother sobbing into a dish towel while Leo raged. "A married man?!" he bellowed. "What kind of fool are you?!"

"I didn't know," Cecilia pleaded, tears streaking her face. "I swear I didn't know! But Daddy, there's something else." She paused, the words catching in her throat. She lowered her voice. "I'm going to have his child."

Leo's fury was uncontrollable, and Concetta clutched her chest and sobbed even louder into her dish towel. Junior was almost as enraged as his father and threatened to go after James. Linda, in shock at hearing about the baby for the first time, wept for her sister.

"You've disgraced this family!" Leo roared so loudly and harshly that Cecilia didn't recognize it.

Cecilia was forbidden from ever seeing James again. Leo went to James's home and told him about the pregnancy. He threatened James with his boxer's fists, doing what he believed any good father had a duty to do. "I'll beat you senseless if you ever come near my daughter again," Leo vowed.

But Leo's threats solved little. There was still the baby. Cecilia's parents couldn't allow her to have an abortion—it was against the Church and illegal on top of that. And Cecilia didn't have it in her heart to terminate the pregnancy, even if she were able to find a midwife or doctor to perform one in secret.

When Cecilia started showing, her parents sent her away to live with distant cousins in upstate New York for a few months, to hide their shame from their neighbors. Yet even as Cecilia's world crumbled, even as she carried this child in secret, her heart still belonged to James. She had faith that she would see him again one day, that he'd leave his wife for her, that they'd become a perfect family. She held onto that dream throughout her pregnancy.

On March 30, 1967, Cecilia awoke to the sterile smell of the hospital, her body aching, her throat dry. Blinking against the fluorescent lights, she turned her head and saw Linda sitting beside her with red-rimmed eyes.

After close to fifteen hours of labor—medicated into a twilight state—Cecilia had given birth to a beautiful 6 pound, 12 ounce baby. She didn't remember much about the experience, but she remembered that her child was a girl.

"Where is she?" Cecilia's voice was quiet and raspy.

Linda hesitated, glancing toward the door. "Cecilia, it's done."

Tears welled in Cecilia's eyes. "No! Please! I didn't even get to hold her."

Linda reached for her sister's hand, squeezing it tightly. "I'm so sorry. I—I didn't want to, but Ma and Daddy. . ."

Cecilia shook her head, silent sobs wracking her body. She felt empty and hollow. "Did she cry?"

Linda swallowed hard. "She did. Just for a moment. But she's so beautiful, Cecilia. She has big brown eyes and a full head of dark hair."

Cecilia turned her head away, staring at the ceiling. "I'll never forgive them." She lay in her hospital bed, feeling like a shell of herself. Her parents had made a choice for her—had taken a choice from her—and she was suffocated by it. She had imagined cradling her baby, cooing promises into her tiny ears, but now there was only a hollow ache.

Linda pressed her forehead against their joined hands. "Neither will I."

The days after leaving the hospital blurred together. Cecilia moved through them in a haze, barely speaking, barely eating. She was back in her childhood bedroom now, but everything felt foreign, like she had been dropped back into a life that no longer belonged to her. Her mother tried to console her in the only way she knew how by cooking her favorite meals and insisting she eat, but Cecilia had no appetite.

With a bond that only twins can have, Linda was the only one who seemed to understand. She sat beside her sister in silence whenever Cecilia couldn't bring herself to speak, which was most of the time. Cecilia inherently understood that Linda was grieving too. Linda had lost a niece, but she kept her hurt to herself—for Cecilia's sake.

"You need to get out of this house," Linda said one evening as they sat on the stoop, the city lights sparkling above. "Go somewhere. Do something. Just—anything other than wasting away here."

Cecilia knew Linda was right, but nothing mattered anymore, so what was the point? She had carried her baby, felt her tiny kicks, and dreamed of holding her, but in the end, her baby had been snatched away like none of it ever happened.

James came around the neighborhood a few days later. He tracked Cecilia down at the Italian deli on the corner. He hadn't seen her since before the birth, and when she looked at him, she barely recognized him. He looked different—guilt in his eyes, hesitation in his step.

"I'm sorry," he said.

Cecilia scoffed. "For what? For lying to me? For leaving me to deal with this alone? For not claiming your own child?"

James exhaled sharply. "I didn't know what to do, Cecilia. My whole life was a mess, and your father threatened me. My marriage was falling apart, and—"

"—Your marriage," she spat. "You should've told me from the beginning."

"I know," he admitted, running a hand through his hair. "I was a coward."

Cecilia turned away, staring at a row of olive oil bottles on a shelf. "It doesn't matter now," she lied.

James reached out and touched her hand, and despite her grief, shame, and anger, she didn't pull away. When he asked her to walk around the block with him, some secret part of her heart jumped. When he told her he was divorcing his wife and that he loved her and wanted to be with her, she let herself believe him. And a month later when he asked her to run away with him to Florida for a fresh start, she packed her bags.

∞ ∞ ∞

Cecilia and James were pronounced husband and wife only weeks after they moved into their small Jacksonville apartment. It was a quick and quiet courthouse ceremony with no family and only one witness. It was nothing like the elaborate, traditional celebration that Cecilia had always dreamed of.

As a contractor by trade, James didn't find it hard to find year-round work. He promised Cecilia a new and happy life, but he was always working, always out. She spent long, lonely days in their apartment, waiting for him to come home, mourning her lost daughter, and pretending she wasn't unraveling.

Within weeks, she found out she was pregnant again. The news should have sent joy rippling through her entire being, but instead, it terrified her. What if James left her? What if she lost this baby too? What if she wasn't strong enough to do this again?

Cecilia didn't tell anyone back home about the child right away, not even Linda. No one in her family was a fan of her marriage, and she didn't know how they'd react to another child, especially one so soon.

On March 11, 1968, Cecilia gave birth to a baby boy. The delivery was easier than her first one, and the medication didn't leave her in so much of a daze. She named her son Carmine Leo after her grandfather and father. This time, no one snatched her baby away. She was a respectable woman now with a married name—Esposito—not merely a girl who'd gotten herself in trouble. When she held her son in her arms, she promised she would never let him go.

Cecilia loved her son fiercely, but with his every feeding and diaper change, every gurgle or yawn, she was reminded of the daughter she'd lost. Her love for Carmine and the emptiness of losing her firstborn pitted themselves against each other deep inside of her, and balancing her joy and her hurt clawed into her very soul with talons sharper than a sword.

Although James was oblivious to Cecilia's hurt, he was sweet on the baby. He held him every night after work. On weekends, he let Cecilia sleep in. But that didn't last long. Before Carmine could even sit up on his own, James began leaving Cecilia alone for long stretches of time. Soon, rumors swirled—other women, gambling, trouble Cecilia didn't want to know about. When she confronted him, he shrugged it off. "This is just how life is, Cecilia."

It wasn't long before their fights turned ugly. They were no longer blissful newlyweds, and the tension between them grew. Cecilia demanded something more, something better than James was giving her and their son. She'd been raised to know how a husband should behave, and it wasn't this.

"You think I don't know what you're doing when you disappear for two days?" Cecilia hissed, blocking the doorway with her arms crossed. "You smell like smoke and perfume, James. You think I'm stupid?"

James threw his keys onto the table with a clatter. "You don't know anything," he snapped. "You sit here all day in this apartment, clinging to that baby like he's your savior. Maybe if you looked at me the way you used—"

"—Don't you dare blame this on me," she spat. "I gave up everything for this family, for you. And you—you disappear like a ghost. What kind of father are you?"

James laughed bitterly, the sound chilling her. "A better one than I had. And that's the best you're getting."

Enraged, Cecilia picked up a glass from the counter, gripped it until her knuckles went white, and then set it back down with a trembling hand. "Then maybe Carmine deserves better than both of us."

James turned away without another word and slammed the door so hard behind him that the walls shook. Cecilia stood in the silence that followed, her arms wrapped tightly around herself, blinking back tears as Carmine stirred in the next room.

The fights continued, one mixing into the other. It was always the same argument, and James never budged. When he stopped coming home at night, Cecilia had had enough. Desperate, she pushed her hurt farther down. She packed up their son and returned to Brooklyn, determined to give Carmine the life James could never give him.

CHAPTER 2:
STEPHANIE (1967)

Her heels clicked against the worn tile floor in the hallway of the Bensonhurst apartment building. In her arms was a baby girl, barely a week old, wrapped snugly in a donated, hand-knit blanket. The social worker from Catholic Charities found the apartment she needed, knocked twice on the door, and waited.

The door opened slowly. "Mrs. Pellegrino?" the social worker asked.

Angelina Pellegrino, her eyes wide and her breath caught in her throat, could only nod in reply.

"This is her," the social worker said gently. "Born March 30th, 6 pounds, 12 ounces. She's healthy. Strong. She was born here in Brooklyn, in this very neighborhood."

Entranced by the sleeping baby and almost without realizing it, Angelina held out her arms to receive her new daughter. The social worker shifted the baby carefully into the new mother's waiting arms. For a moment, the apartment became completely still except for the ticking of the clock on the mantle, which read five minutes before noon. Angelina stared down at the tiny face nestled beneath the knit cap, her lips trembling with the new love surging through her.

"I—I don't know what to say," she whispered, joyful tears slipping down her cheeks.

"You don't have to say anything," the social worker said kindly, her voice soft. "She's yours now."

The baby let out a quiet sigh as if the sound of her new mother's heartbeat had settled her. Angelina pressed her lips to the baby's forehead. "Stephanie," she murmured. "My Stephanie."

With a glow in her eyes, the social worker handed over a thin envelope with the paperwork inside. Then she showed herself out, stepping back into the hallway. The door closed behind her with a soft click.

Angelina had waited for this moment her entire married life. After years of miscarriages, monthly disappointments, heartbreak, and prayers said into the darkness, she was finally holding her miracle—her Stephanie. Breathless, the new mother wept even as she beamed more brightly than she ever had. She raised her head upward in worship, offering prayers of thanksgiving to the Lord who had delivered this baby to her. Angelina brushed a kiss across Stephanie's forehead, breathing in the powdery scent of her newborn skin. The baby stirred slightly but remained asleep, her tiny fingers curled into a fist.

In the weeks that followed, the natural transition of becoming the family they were always meant to be was set in motion. Most days, the hum of a lullaby filled the small, warm apartment as Angelina rocked her infant daughter in her arms.

One evening after work, Angelina's husband, Jack, entered the nursery, his work boots heavy against the wooden floor. He was a machinist, his hands calloused and worn, but they softened the moment he reached for his daughter who was wrapped in a pink blanket. "How's my princess?" he murmured, taking the baby into his arms. Stephanie stirred, her tiny mouth opening in a yawn. Jack chuckled. "Just like her mother—loves her sleep."

Their home—a second-floor walk-up in Bensonhurst—was small but filled with love. A crucifix hung over the doorway, family photos lined the walls, and the aroma of fresh marinara sauce simmered on the stove. Sundays were sacred—not just for church but for family. After morning Mass, the entire family always gathered at Angelina's sister's house where cousins ran barefoot in the backyard and the adults sipped espresso, speaking in a blend of English and Italian. Adored and cherished, Stephanie was passed from one pair of loving arms to another.

As she grew, Stephanie blossomed into a bright, curious toddler. She had big brown eyes that sparkled with mischief and a laugh that could light up a room. Angelina enrolled her in ballet at the age of three, dressing her in pink tutus and tying her hair into buns. Every year Stephanie was the lead in the year-end recital.

Jack often took Stephanie to the park on Saturdays, pushing her on the swings until she was soaring, her giggles ringing through the air. Her bedroom was a haven with a canopy bed, lace-trimmed pillows, and porcelain dolls. Despite Jack's more modest wages, Stephanie always had the best dresses and the newest toys. Most importantly, she had the unwavering devotion of parents who adored her.

One cousin, Maria, became Stephanie's closest companion as they grew up. Born just a few months apart, they were inseparable. If one was invited to a birthday party, the other went too. If one was in trouble, the other was usually involved. They giggled through Catholic school together, sitting side by side in their plaid skirts and polished Mary Janes, giggling behind their textbooks. They shared secrets, dreams, and the occasional mischief.

Yet despite Stephanie's charmed life, shadows followed her—whispers and signs that something wasn't quite right. It was the way her Aunt Arlene paused mid-sentence when someone commented that Stephanie didn't look much like her parents. At a family barbecue, someone once mumbled, "She's got those eyes—not like Angelina's though," just loud enough for nearby ears to hear. At the family Christmas party, another relative once joked, "You sure she's not Dorothy's kid?" but no one laughed. It was the way certain relatives cast sorrowful glances at her, as if they saw someone else in her features—someone they weren't supposed to speak of. And then there were the missing pieces: no pictures of Angelina pregnant, no stories of Stephanie's birth, no framed photos of one-day-old Stephanie still in the hospital.

Stephanie was eight years old when she first felt it—an unease, a question she didn't yet have the words to ask. Too young to understand but following her instincts, she sat cross-legged on the floor one evening, flipping through an old photo album. She looked up at her mother. "Mommy, how come there aren't any pictures of you when I was in your belly?"

Angelina's hands froze on the dish she was drying. A brief flicker of something—panic maybe—flashed across her face before she forced a grin. "Oh, sweetheart, I didn't like taking pictures when I was pregnant. I'd lost babies before you because God needed them in Heaven. I was so scared I'd lose you too. I didn't want to jinx it."

Stephanie accepted the explanation, at least for a while. Over the years, she asked the question again, phrased in different ways, and her mother always had the same answer. But the feeling that something wasn't quite right never went away. It lingered in the pit of her stomach, a murmur in the back of her mind that grew louder as she got older.

As Stephanie moved into adolescence, she found herself caught between the girl she had always been and the unsettling feeling that had become part of her life. The doubts that had been mere whispers in her childhood became louder—no longer fleeting thoughts but now gnawing suspicions.

Stephanie began to notice the cracks. She saw how her mother grew tense whenever the topic of pregnancy or childbirth came up. She watched as Angelina changed the subject, her voice too bright, her smile too forced. And she saw how her father, usually so strong and steady, would shift uncomfortably whenever Stephanie asked about the day she was born. Yet she'd seen her birth certificate with her own eyes. Issued by the State of New York, it had her parents' names on it, and the seal was embossed. Yet even that official document didn't quell her uneasiness.

Thankfully, there was dance. Dancing gave Stephanie the kind of euphoria that no words could express. Ballet turned into tap, then jazz, and when she danced, she became weightless, utterly alive with every move. Each step made her feel like she could rise above the world itself.

Her dream sharpened early. She wanted to attend the famed School of Performing Arts in Manhattan and become a professional dancer. She practiced for hours in the living room, balancing on the hardwood floor, mimicking the elegance of the women she saw on TV. Her parents encouraged her, especially Jack who loved showing her off to anyone who would watch her twirl. Dance felt like destiny, like something that would one day carry her out of Brooklyn and into something bigger, like something that would quell the gnawing once and for all.

∞ ∞ ∞

When Stephanie was thirteen, she came home from school one afternoon, and her parents told her to sit down in the kitchen, even before she could change out of her uniform. Her father was almost never home in the afternoons, and almost instinctively, Stephanie knew her world was about to crack open.

Jack was sick. Pancreatic cancer.

The illness came fast. Jack tried to fight, to be strong for his family, but the sickness ravaged him, and Stephanie could only watch as her father shrank. His voice, once thunderous, became coarse and tiny. When Father Dominic came to give Jack his Last Rites, Stephanie sat at the edge of her father's bed and screamed at the priest to get out—God wasn't taking her daddy, not now, not if she could help it.

But God did. Within a year, Jack was gone. Stephanie's heart ripped open, the void too much for a fourteen-year-old girl to bear. Nothing could fill it—not her mother's love, not the years of memories she had, not cousin Maria's hugs and shared tears. Angelina did her best—Mass, meatballs, long talks with her daughter—but grief settled over their household, touching everything, changing everything.

Stephanie began to change too. The structure and security that once defined her life was gone, and suddenly her upbringing felt like a cage. She rebelled in small ways at first—wearing too much makeup, not doing her chores, handing her homework in late. Then she started slipping out the back door of her apartment building after curfew, with Maria in tow. One Friday night when they were just fifteen, they jumped the turnstile at the 18th Avenue station, giggling as they clutched each other's hands, and headed into Manhattan.

"Steph, your mom's gonna kill you," Maria said as they slipped into a crowded downtown club, their fake IDs still warm from the printer.

"Let her try," Stephanie muttered, her eyes glittering beneath smudged eyeliner as the beat of the music pulsed in her chest. When she stepped onto the dance floor for the first time—surrounded by strangers, sweat, and strobe lights—she felt untouchable. Free.

It was the 1980s, and New York City became their playground. Stephanie and Maria snuck out more and more often. For those few hours in Manhattan, with music and dance engulfing her, Stephanie wasn't the girl haunted by unspoken secrets. She wasn't the daughter without a father or the girl who didn't quite fit. She was just herself—wild, reckless, and alive. She could drown out the questions and the hurt with music, with laughter, with rebellion.

But when the music stopped, she still longed for answers. And now, beneath her questions, a new anger simmered—anger at her father for leaving, anger at her mother for growing brittle with grief, and anger at God for shattering the world she once believed in.

That world was gone in so many ways. Without Jack's wages, finances at home grew tighter and tighter as their savings diminished. Angelina got an unskilled factory job, but her earnings weren't enough to carry them. By the time Stephanie was seventeen, the unpaid bills towered around them, and Angelina had to accept help from her family. Stephanie's dreams of professional dance died. There was no money for lessons or auditions, and with her father gone, there was no one to push her anymore, no one to make her sparkle.

The future that Stephanie had imagined dissolved into nothingness. College was no longer an option. As soon as she was eighteen, she began taking the train into Manhattan and temping wherever she could—law offices, reception desks, executive suites. She moved fast, she learned fast, and even though it meant opening a charge account at Macy's, she dressed the part.

While her friends who'd gone off to college were still figuring out their majors, Stephanie landed a job as a legal assistant and made decent money. She didn't have a degree, but she had grit. Street smarts. Brooklyn fire. She often said she felt like the man of the house, always the one stepping in, stepping up, holding things together. Her sense of duty, combined with the sharp edge of grief and her lingering suspicions, shaped her into a woman who could stand strong.

∞ ∞ ∞

Still in her work clothes, Stephanie walked down the hall and knocked on her neighbor's door. "Lidia, are you home?"

The older woman with her gray curls opened the door. "Stephanie, honey, come in."

Stephanie stepped into the small, tidy apartment. Lidia had lived in the building for as long as Stephanie could remember, and she'd been her mother's bosom friend since well before Stephanie was born. Lidia was often present at holiday gatherings and any Sunday dinners that Stephanie's mother hosted.

"My mother made you some anise cookies," Stephanie said as she stepped into the apartment and handed the tin of cookies to Lidia.

Lidia invited her to stay for a bit and then put the cookies on a plate for them to share. "Anise cookies are my favorite," Lidia said, although Stephanie already knew that. Stephanie had adored her as a child—adored her still—and she knew most of Lidia's favorites.

Lidia took the chair across from Stephanie. She studied her guest for a long moment, and then her eyes turned wistful. "You're growing up so fast," Lidia said softly. "You remind me so much of someone I used to know."

Stephanie tilted her head, a spark of excitement shooting through her. "Who?"

Lidia hesitated before shaking her head. "Oh, it's nothing, dear. Just an old woman's memories."

But Stephanie had seen it—the flicker of something behind Lidia's eyes, something left unsaid. And for the first time, Stephanie realized that maybe, just maybe, she wasn't imagining things after all.

CHAPTER 3:
Carmine
(1968)

Cecilia stood on the familiar stoop of her red-brick, childhood home, a worn suitcase in one hand, Carmine cradled in her other arm. The baby's whimpers barely covered the pounding of her heart.

Linda answered the door, opening it just a crack at first. "You came!" Linda cried, pulling her twin into a hug that smelled of coffee and Jean Naté perfume. "I told you—I will always be here for you. Come in. We'll figure things out."

Cecilia pushed down her tears and stepped inside. Her father sat in his armchair in the corner of the living room, his newspaper lowered just enough to reveal his steely glare. He didn't speak. He didn't have to. The judgment in his eyes pressed down harder than words ever could.

"Don't start, Daddy," Linda said, intercepting his scowl. "She's home now."

Cecilia glanced down at Carmine and then back at her father. "I just want to do right by him," she said. Leo grunted, folding his paper with exaggerated care before leaving the room without a word.

Linda led her sister to the small bedroom they'd shared as girls. Cecilia began unpacking in silence while Linda sat on the edge of her bed, bouncing Carmine gently in her arms. "He looks like us," Linda said. "Poor thing."

Cecilia gave a tired laugh. "God help him then." Sighing, she looked around her old bedroom with resignation. "And God help us."

Now that Cecilia was back in her childhood home, she began trying to rebuild her life, but the weight of her past never let her rest. She adored Carmine—he was her anchor, the only good thing that had come from her disastrous marriage to James. She rocked her son to sleep at night, held him tight when the memories of his sister haunted her thoughts, and strove to be a good mother. She tried—tried hard—but she still had to fight to keep her demons at bay. She struggled with the loss of her daughter, the estrangement from her husband, and the future that James should have given her and their children.

Cecilia did her best, knowing that her life wasn't just about her anymore. Thankfully, her family quickly softened to their innocent new addition. Her mother helped with the diaper changes and bottle warmings, and hummed old lullabies to Carmine in Italian. Her father remained gruff, but he built Carmine a crib with his own hands, often muttering about sanding each slat smooth or saying things like this: "The kid needs something solid in his life, unlike what he's had so far."

Cecilia's brother, Junior, who had moved out not long after Cecilia ran off, would swing by after work to visit the baby and bounce him on his knee. Linda made sure Cecilia ate, showered, and got a few hours of sleep each night. "You're not doing this alone," Linda told her every so often, always placing a firm hand on her sister's shoulder. "We won't let you."

Yet Carmine's home was filled with contradictions. His mother was fervently devoted to him, but her heartache made her reckless. Trying to dull her pain, she drank too much, took too many pills, and cried too often. When she was at her worst, Linda or their mother stepped in without question—pulling Carmine into their arms, distracting him with stories and his favorite treats, and showering him with attention. "He doesn't need to see you like this, Cecilia," her mother would say gently. "Go lie down. I've got him."

On Cecilia's good days, she was full of life, singing along to the radio as she cooked, sharing her warm smiles freely, and wrapping Carmine in tight hugs. When he was old enough, she began taking him for walks along the avenue where she'd buy him Italian ices and tell him stories about her childhood.

One afternoon, as she and Carmine sat on a stoop licking cherry and lemon ices from paper cups, Cecilia pointed to a faded mural on the side of a hardware store. "That used to be Mr. Romano's café," she said. "I worked there one summer when I was fifteen. I once burned my hand on the espresso machine and cried in the walk-in freezer so no one would see me." She laughed a little and then added, "He gave me a pignoli cookie to make up for it. Said I was tough for a girl." Carmine, only four years old, listened wide-eyed, imagining his mother as a teenager, brave and stubborn even then. In those small moments, Cecilia was the best mother a boy could ask for. She read him bedtime stories, cooked his favorite foods, and made him laugh with her affections.

∞ ∞ ∞

By the time Carmine was old enough to start understanding the world around him, he'd learned to navigate his mother's instability. He knew when to be quiet, when to comfort her, and when to disappear into his own world of comic books and baseball cards.

He excelled in school. A bright, observant child, he was quick to pick up on things others missed. Smart and quick-witted, he had a natural charm that made him well-liked by his teachers and classmates alike. Yet he carried a sadness in him, a feeling that something was missing, though he didn't yet know what.

Carmine was only seven when he first realized that his family wasn't like the others in his neighborhood. His friends all had fathers who took them to ball games, taught them how to ride bikes, and sat with them at the dinner table each night. And most of his friends had plenty of siblings and didn't live with their aunts and grandparents. While Carmine loved his family, he saw that his mother was different, and he wondered why.

It wasn't long before Carmine wandered into the kitchen one evening, the sun still bright in the summer sky, to where Cecilia sat at the table, swirling the last of her wine in a chipped glass. The pungent smell of garlic was in the air, even though the stove had gone cold hours ago.

"Mommy," he asked cautiously, climbing onto the chair across from her, "how come I don't have a dad like Mikey or Paulie?"

Cecilia blinked, caught off guard. She took a slow sip from her glass and then set it down a little too hard. "You've got *me*, sweetheart," she said with a smile that didn't reach her eyes. "And you've got all of us. That's more than enough, ain't it?"

"But where is he?" Carmine pressed. "Did he go somewhere?"

Her expression darkened, and Carmine cowered just a bit. She stood up abruptly, wiping her hands on a dish towel even though they weren't dirty or wet. "He's gone, Carmine. That's all you need to know."

"But why?" he asked, insisting. "All the other kids have fathers." He hesitated and added in a smaller voice, "Was it something I did?"

Cecilia froze for a moment, her back to him. Then she turned, her face tight. "No, baby. It wasn't you." Her voice was low. "It was never you."

He looked up at her, his eyes wide. "Was it something *you* did then?"

Cecilia's breath caught. "Enough!" she snapped, speaking more sharply than she'd meant to. Softening, she crouched beside him. "You don't need a father to be somebody. You're gonna be just fine without him. You hear me?"

Carmine nodded slowly, knowing this was a moment when he should go read his comic books. But that didn't mean the question was answered, and it stayed with him.

With his world at home sometimes too confusing, Carmine found solace in baseball. He idolized the players he saw on TV, fantasizing about the day he would step onto a Major League field. The neighborhood sandlot became the place where he felt most like himself, the one place where all the noise in his life faded away. He played many afternoons until the streetlights came on, practicing his swing and perfecting his pitch.

"Back up, back up! Carmine's up!" one of the boys shouted from center field. Carmine stepped into the batter's box, his sneakers scuffed, his knuckles white on the taped bat handle. The sun dipped low behind the chain-link fence, casting long shadows across the infield. Joey wound up and fired a pitch, and Carmine's eyes locked on the ball. *Crack!* The sound of wood smacking against leather echoed down the block.

"Run!" shouted his teammates.

Carmine took off, legs pumping, dust kicking up behind his heels. He rounded first base and then second. Glancing over his shoulder, he saw the ball bounce off the right-field fence—there was just enough time to run. As he slid into third, cheers erupted from his teammates. Carmine grinned, his chest heaving.

"A triple!" Vinnie shouted, his arms raised. "Told you he's got rocket legs."

Taking in the moment for a second, Carmine looked up at the sky, his heart still pounding. Here in the sandlot, on the field, it was just him, the bat, the ball, and the dream that maybe, just maybe, he could play pro someday. Here he didn't have to think about his mother's moods, his father's absence, or the questions he harbored.

As Carmine entered seventh grade, he started to realize that trouble was everywhere on the streets of Brooklyn. Not everyone in Bensonhurst came from hardworking, law-abiding families like his. There were plenty of petty criminals and old-school tough guys who demanded respect for the streets they ruled. He started seeing kids get mixed up in things that led to nowhere but trouble. He began hearing of high school guys getting girls pregnant, of hoodlums amassing rap sheets. His grandfather especially had instilled in him the importance of staying out of trouble, of being a "real man," so Carmine learned to stand his ground in any situation. He was determined not to become a street thug, but the temptation was always there. Sometimes when everything felt wrong, he thought it would be easy to cast off his home life and disappear into the streets.

His mother, despite her struggles, fought to keep him on the right path. Cecilia warned him about the dangers and the consequences. "You're better than this life, Carmine," she'd say, her voice slurred from one too many drinks but her love for him still unmistakable. And to Carmine, his mother was still the most beautiful, strongest woman in the world, even if life had worn her down in ways he didn't fully understand. He made a promise to himself: Someday he would care for her the way she had tried to take care of him.

But then came Sundays, the day of the week when even promises felt impossible. On Sundays, Cecilia would sleep late, her eyes rimmed with sorrow after the previous Saturday night. Sometimes she wouldn't get out of bed at all, and the whole house felt heavier.

"Cecilia, come on," Linda pleaded one Sunday, nudging her sister's shoulder through the twisted sheets. "Ma's making sauce, and Daddy's been pacing the kitchen since breakfast. We have to get going to twelve o'clock Mass."

Cecilia groaned, her arm flopping over her eyes to block the light. "Tell her I'm sick. I have a headache."

Linda didn't flinch. "You told her that last Sunday—and the Sunday before. Now come on, get up. Father Sal has been asking after you."

Carmine, an incoming freshman in high school and tall for his age, stood in the doorway, already dressed for Mass in his button-down shirt and slacks, his hair combed the way his nonna liked it. His dark eyes were shadowed with frustration. "You said we'd go today," he said flatly. "You promised."

Cecilia winced. Slowly, she shifted, her eyes bloodshot and heavy with sleep. Like most Saturday evenings, she'd been out partying all night with yet another man who wouldn't stay around for long.

"You look handsome, baby," she told Carmine, her voice scratchy and heavy with regret and too much red wine. Carmine grinned at the compliment, but when Cecilia didn't move to get up and instead rested her hand on her forehead again, the light in his face dimmed.

Linda rolled her eyes but softened. "He needs you. And you need to shower. Come downstairs when you're human."

Carmine stayed behind a moment longer, staring at his mother. Her hair was tangled and her makeup smeared, but to him she still looked like the woman who used to sing to him in the kitchen.

Cecilia exhaled and leaned back. "I'll be right there, sweetheart," she said. "I just need ten more minutes." Carmine didn't look convinced, but he started down the hall, leaving the door open behind him.

∞ ∞ ∞

Carmine soon received his Confirmation, and with age, he started asking more and more questions about his father. One evening after a particularly bad day, Cecilia unexpectedly sat him down at the kitchen table. Cigarette smoke clung to the air, mixing with the faint scent of whiskey from her glass. She ran a hand through her dark hair and sighed.

"I know you wonder about your father," she said suddenly.

Stunned, Carmine sat upright. "Yeah," he admitted.

Cecilia stared at him for a long moment before shaking her head. "He wasn't a good man," she said, the same words she always used. But this time, her voice cracked a little. "He lied when it mattered, and he hurt the people who loved him. He made promises he never kept." She looked away as if the memories were too sharp to hold. "But you—you are nothing like him. I want you to know that."

Carmine wasn't sure what to say, so he just kept listening.

"You're getting older now, I understand, but don't go looking for him," she said, her voice suddenly harsher. "Promise me."

Carmine looked at her, his jaw tight. "Why not? Why shouldn't I find him?" he asked almost inaudibly. "Don't I deserve to know?"

Cecilia's eyes flickered with something—fear maybe, or shame. She reached for her glass but didn't drink. "Some truths don't make anything better," she said. "They just make you bleed in places no one can see."

Carmine considered her words. He shrugged.

"Promise me," Cecilia repeated, softer this time.

But Carmine didn't promise. He couldn't. By now he understood that he needed to know who his father was, needed to know where the other half of him came from. Deep down, he knew that one day when he was old enough, he would set out to find answers for himself.

CHAPTER 4:

Across the Expanse (1983)

"I'm not going to Hawaii!" Carmine's voice sliced through the cigarette haze, sharp as an icy gust sneaking through a cracked window.

Cecilia froze for a moment. She turned from the kitchen sink, a dish towel clutched in her hand. "What do you mean you're not going?" Her voice was tight, not from anger but from disbelief. "We've talked about this."

"No. *You* talked." Carmine spat. "*You* made this decision, not me."

"You're fifteen!" she said.

"I know how old I am. I'm also not an idiot," Carmine snapped. "I'm old enough to know I don't want to live with that guy. And you shouldn't either."

Cecilia's chest tightened. She gripped the towel harder than necessary. "Victor's giving us a chance—a new life."

"You really expect me to go with you? With that piece of garbage? He's nothing but a drunk mechanic with a temper."

"Watch your mouth!" she snapped.

"So anyone who claims to love you gets a pass?" Carmine continued, his voice louder now. "He gave you a bruised cheek and a busted kitchen cabinet just last week. Some chance!" He slammed his palm on the table, a thwack that echoed through the kitchen. "You think I'm gonna move five thousand miles away and pretend he's God's gift to the world?"

Cecilia's relationship with Victor had started off like a patch of spring grass after a long, frozen winter. Laughs at the bar. Worn hands that fixed things. Compliments that felt like truths—not like the false platitudes that she spoke into the mirror just to get through the mornings.

"It's not that simple, Carmine. He's not always like that. He's the first man to love me in fifteen years." The words spilled out before she could stop them. They sounded pitiful, even to her.

Carmine stared at his mother for a long moment, like he didn't recognize her anymore. "You call that love? I'm not going, Ma. I'll stay here with Nonna and Papa."

Cecilia's hand shook as she reached for her cigarettes on the counter. "Fine! I can't force you. You're old enough to make your own decision."

The front door creaked open. Cecilia glanced in that direction. Her voice tight, she said, "He's here. Please, just . . . don't—"

Victor's boots scraped along the floor, his heavy frame casting a shadow that swallowed the last sliver of the day's sunlight. "What did I just walk in on?" he asked, smelling of engine oil and something heavier. His words were thick with bourbon.

"We were just talking," Cecilia said quickly.

Victor turned to Carmine. "You still mad about last week?"

Carmine stiffened. "Your girlfriend wants to drag me to Hawaii like a stray dog," he snapped.

Victor let out a bitter laugh. "That's what this is about?" He stepped closer. "You're fifteen, kid. You're not a man. You got a job? You got a house? You think you're staying in Brooklyn while your mother starts over? You don't get a say in this."

Carmine squared his shoulders. "I'm man enough to recognize when someone is dangerous. You're not taking me anywhere."

Victor's eyes flared, fists clenched. "You little punk!" He lunged forward. Cecilia stepped in, but the movement came too fast. Victor's knuckles grazed her shoulder, shoved her aside, and then curled toward Carmine's jaw—not landing hard but more like a punctuation, brutal and final.

"Carmine!" she cried. "Victor, don't you touch him!" Cecilia screamed, stepping between them, her hand pressed against Victor's chest.

Carmine staggered back, blood starting to pool at his lip. His chest heaved, and he looked directly at Cecilia. His eyes narrowed, not in pain but from betrayal. "I'm done, Ma," he said, walking toward the door. She moved to stop him, but he already had his hand on the doorknob.

Carmine paused on his way out. "You chose him. Remember that," he said without looking back. He slammed the door behind him.

That night at Victor's apartment, after he'd passed out, Cecilia sat on the edge of the bed, holding the phone between two shaking hands. The line rang, rang, rang, and then finally someone picked up. Linda didn't even say hello. She just said, "I've got him." Cecilia inhaled. "He's hurt," Linda added. "Not just the lip. You know that, right?"

"I never wanted this," Cecilia said softly.

"You did," Linda said gently. "Just not like this."

A week later, Cecilia left. No tears, no goodbye letter, no long embraces—just a suitcase, a plane ticket, and her son staring out the window as the cab pulled away.

With Cecilia gone, the house felt too big. It still smelled of lemon Pledge and old upholstery, and Carmine's nonna, Concetta, started making his bed every morning, even though he told her not to. Papa grumbled about the Giants and let Carmine sip wine at dinner. Without Cecilia's wild whirlwind, everything seemed ordinary—a quiet, dependable existence.

Yet none of it erased the truth. Carmine's mother had left, and it consumed him. Every night he thought of his abandonment as he lay stiffly on his twin mattress, his eyes fixed on the wobbling ceiling fan. Sleep always hovered above him, too far away.

One night he sat on the stoop with his Aunt Linda, the late-spring air thick with humidity. She said, "Your mom used to do my hair when we were little. We would sit out here and eat lemon Italian ices, and she'd braid my hair. Life was simple."

"She really left," Carmine said, his voice low.

"Your mom thinks she's surviving," Linda replied, handing him a soda from the cooler.

"She picked him over me," he said, his voice strained and cracking.

"She picked what she thought would fix her," said Linda.

Carmine looked away. "I feel like I've been left behind my whole life."

"She's broken, Carmine. Has been since—well, for a long time. She's carrying things she never put down." Linda reached out, brushing Carmine's hair back with her fingers.

"She told me he was the first man to love her in fifteen years," he said.

"That's not the same as being loved well," Linda soothed. "You're not the one who failed here. You saved yourself." She closed her eyes and took a deep breath. "She loves you."

"Then why did she leave?" he whispered.

"She was drowning. And drowning people don't always recognize the hand reaching for them."

Carmine closed his eyes to fight back the tears, knowing deep in his heart that he couldn't keep someone together who didn't know how to be whole.

"No father. No mother. No sisters, no brothers," Carmine muttered. "Who am I?"

∞ ∞ ∞

Cecilia followed the fantasy and boarded a plane with too many regrets but not enough summer clothes. The plane lifted into the sky while she pressed her forehead against the window, watching Brooklyn shrink until it became a smudge of her past life and hoping Maui would transform into a promise. Victor slept through most of the flight, mouth open, snoring. He was originally from Maui, or so he claimed. He'd always spoken of it as a lost Eden as he sipped whiskey and smelled of car-radiator repairs. He said they would start fresh, build a life. He promised peace under palm trees.

Near the beach they rented a yellow bungalow with tilted porch steps and a busted wind chime. Cecilia unpacked slowly. She placed a Polaroid of Carmine on her nightstand, tucked inside a seashell dish.

The bungalow was close enough to the beach that Cecilia could hear the waves crashing at night. The air smelled sweet, like guava and gardenias, and the mornings made her feel like maybe this was it—maybe this was peace. Maybe this is what hope looked like—palm trees, ocean spray, breezes that didn't carry the scent of sewers.

Victor got a job at a garage. He usually came home late, arms coated in grease. He brought home mangoes and grilled fish for dinner. He called Cecilia "baby" and grinned widely like he did the first week they'd met.

In the evenings, they sat on the porch watching the stars glint like glass shards.

"It's peaceful," she said.

Victor nodded. "It's nice here, huh? No sirens. No city stink."

Amid the tropical paradise, Cecilia tried to reinvent herself. She worked in a bakery two mornings a week and carried home pineapple loaves in wax paper. She found a rhythm. She walked barefoot across the beach and collected smooth stones and sea glass. Her body started to soften, and she reached for the bottle less often. She imagined the weight she carried evaporating into the breeze. Life seemed so good that she almost believed it. She clung to hope. She wanted to believe this place could wash her clean.

Every few weeks she called Carmine. Sometimes he answered. Sometimes he didn't. But when he did, their conversations were stilted, almost forced.

"Hey sweetheart," she'd say.

"Hey," he'd echo.

"How are you doing? How's school? Still playing baseball?"

"Fine, and yes," was Carmine's usual brusque response.

"Nonna said you're eating like a king," Cecilia said nervously, trying to keep the conversation going.

"She exaggerates," replied Carmine.

Silence.

Cecilia wanted to tell him about the sunsets, about how the sky turned lavender so vividly. But Carmine was distant, their connection severed so completely that it was as if it had never existed.

"I miss you, sweetheart." Cecilia's voice was soft.

"I don't know what to do with that," Carmine replied.

Cecilia nodded, even though he couldn't see her. "I love you," she said and then hung up before he could answer. She didn't cry until the receiver was back in the cradle.

By early fall, Victor started coming home from work later and later. The change in Victor was slow, almost imperceptible—beer with dinner, bourbon after work. Slowly, the bitterness crept back in. He drank in the garage, muttered about work, barked about money. He started to drink more than he had in Brooklyn. He screamed over burned rice, accused Cecilia of flirting with the postman, and insulted her weight, her laugh, and her parenting. He said Carmine would have gone with her if she hadn't spoiled him with softness.

"You ever think *you're* the problem?" he once asked, derision in his voice. Feeling defeated, Cecilia didn't fight back. She didn't want to. She was still too broken to believe that something better was out there for her. Eventually, Victor started sleeping on the couch.

Cecilia's cough started the week of Thanksgiving. It was dry but persistent. She ignored it at first, brushing it off as nothing. Then came the chest pain, sharp and constant like something pressing from the inside out. She told herself it was the vog—the volcanic haze locals talked about that hit you like a ghost in the lungs. Victor told her to stop complaining. "It's just a cough, not the end of the world."

She went to the doctor alone. She took the bus, wore sunglasses, and sat silently beneath fluorescent lights. The nurse was gentle, but the scan techs were not. It wasn't the vog.

After weeks of X-rays, bloodwork, a biopsy, and long waits in sterile offices, a doctor finally said the words: lung cancer, stage four. Inoperable. At thirty-five years old, the years Cecilia had spent treating her body like an amusement park had finally caught up with her.

She told no one for six days. Instead, she wrote letters she didn't send, much like the ones she'd written in the past. She folded them carefully and tucked them into her jewelry box. Then she called Carmine.

"I'm sick," she said.

"Flu?" he asked.

"No, worse," said Cecilia.

Carmine didn't respond right away. "What kind of sick?" he asked after a moment, a fearful caution in his voice.

"The kind that doesn't go away. Lung cancer. They said—they said it's bad." She lowered her voice. "I don't know how long I have."

Silence.

Carmine inhaled sharply. "Is someone helping you?"

"Victor's here," she said. "Sometimes."

"Do you want me to come?" he asked.

"No. Not for this," she said softly.

Neither of them spoke for a long time. "I'm sorry," she finally said. "For everything." Carmine didn't reply. She thought he might cry, but the line stayed silent. Eventually, Cecilia hung up.

In the months that followed, the pain grew sharper. She stopped working. The treatment was torturous. Chemicals carved into Cecilia's veins like map lines of remorse, and hair loss came quickly. Soon, she barely left her bed. Neighbors brought soup, but her appetite had vanished. A woman named Maile came to clean twice a week. Sometimes Cecilia forgot her name. It was too hard to think through the fog, the pain, and the regrets.

Victor drifted in and out of their home like a shadow, present only long enough to ask if Cecilia needed a drink of water. He stayed out longer and longer, and sometimes he didn't return home at night. Home hospice care quickly became necessary. With what little strength she had left, Cecilia insisted Victor arrange a priest for her Last Rites.

One night in a morphine haze, she called Carmine again.

"Did you talk to your sister yet?" Cecilia asked.

Carmine frowned, pressing the phone tighter against his ear. "Ma, what are you talking about?"

"Did you talk to your sister yet?" she repeated, her words slow yet blended together, almost incoherent.

"Ma, I don't understand what you're saying."

She let out a sigh, her breath shaky. "Never mind. Forget I said anything."

He thought she was confused. He chalked it up to the drugs, to the sickness that had taken over her body.

Cecilia died in her sleep two weeks later. The little girl who once giggled on 86th Street, who'd fallen in love so recklessly, had been consumed by the sorrow she could never escape. She spent her final moments thinking of the child she'd lost, the daughter who'd never left her heart.

The hospice nurse said the death was quiet, like a tide pulling away. Victor told her he'd handle the remains. He called the cremation service from a bar pay phone, slurring the spelling of her name. No wake. No ceremony. Just a weightless goodbye with her ashes and jewelry box shipped to her family in Brooklyn.

For Carmine, Cecilia's death left yet another hole in his life. But her last words to him—the desperation in her voice, the urgency of it despite her weakness, the hint of truth that rang out just a little too loudly to ignore—also left something else: a question, a mystery, a truth waiting to be uncovered.

CHAPTER 5:

YOUNG OFFENDER (1984)

The phone rang. Leo's heart sank. A call at this time of night on a Sunday was never good, and this was the third time this month.

"Yeah, this is Leo Russo," he grumbled into the receiver.

"Mr. Russo, this is Officer Danvers down at the 62nd Precinct. We've got your grandson here. He's okay, but you'll need to come pick him up."

Leo pinched the bridge of his nose. "What'd he do this time?"

"We caught him and a couple of other boys tagging a storefront on Bay Parkway. Shop owner didn't press charges. He just wants the graffiti cleaned up."

Leo sighed in response, deep and tired. "I'll be there in twenty minutes."

When Leo arrived at the precinct, the door creaked ajar with an understated authority as though the door itself knew better than to announce him. The fluorescent lights in the precinct buzzed—high-pitched and persistent—like mosquitoes gnawing at the quiet.

Carmine sat slouched on the bench, the hoodie he always wore drawn up like armor, his sneakers tapping out a restless rhythm against the linoleum. His knuckles were raw, and one was split open from a fight that hadn't been worth remembering. The clock on the wall ticked toward midnight, and at the desk, the intake officer sighed for the fifth time in as many minutes.

Carmine didn't look up. He knew Papa would come. Eventually.

The precinct was three blocks from the old De-Luxe movie theater on Bath Avenue that Carmine had ducked behind when the shopkeeper called the cops. Dumb move. The whole night had been dumb, actually. Paulie had just scored a case of spray paint, and he thought tagging his way through Bensonhurst was a great idea. A voice in Carmine's head had said, *Do it.* For most of his life, he would have heard a competing voice—his mother's—urging him home, but Cecilia had gone quiet in his mind months ago.

Leo, with his great stature, moved as if he were made of brick. Carmine finally lifted his head. Leo stood there in wrinkled slacks and a cardigan that fit too snugly. He didn't speak. He just stared. His nostrils flared slightly, the harsh light of the precinct glinting off his combed-back silver hair.

Leo's eyes scanned the room and landed on Carmine. The intake cop handed Leo a clipboard. "You his grandfather?" the officer asked.

Leo nodded once.

"Sign here." The officer pointed to the form on the clipboard.

Leo signed without speaking.

"He's over there." The officer pointed right. "Same crew. Nobody hurt. Just kids being stupid."

Leo nodded curtly and then walked over to his grandson. "Get up."

Carmine didn't move.

Leo leaned in, his voice low and sharp. "I said get up!"

Carmine followed him out into the night, shoulders hunched, with the precinct's metal door clanging shut behind them. The ride home was silent until they were two blocks from the house.

"What the heck is wrong with you?" Leo finally barked, gripping the wheel like it might break. "You wanna end up like those punks down on 24th Avenue selling dime bags and getting stabbed in stairwells? You're lucky Mr. Santucci didn't press charges."

Carmine only stared out the window, his jaw clenched.

"Nonna cries herself to sleep over you. You know that?" Leo asked.

Still nothing.

"You think you're the only one who lost something when your mother died?" Leo continued.

Something inside Carmine shifted painfully. "She left me, Papa," he said hoarsely. "She left me even before she died, and now she's never coming back."

Leo didn't respond. As he pulled the Buick into the driveway, the porch light spilled over the rosebush that Concetta had planted last summer. She was sleeping, probably with rosary beads clutched to her chest. Many nights she fell asleep while saying prayers for a boy who'd stopped believing in anything.

Leo turned in his seat. "You think anyone in this house has the luxury of giving up? You think Nonna gave up when your mother died?" he asked.

Carmine stared back, defiant. "I didn't ask to be saved."

Leo's voice sharpened again. "No, but your nonna still tries. I still try. And every time you throw your fists at the world like it owes you something, you make it harder for people to love you."

Carmine exhaled, long and slow. "Maybe that's the point."

"Be quiet going into the house. Take care of that hand, and then go straight to bed," Leo said, his voice low. "You'll face your nonna tomorrow."

Carmine didn't go to his room. After Leo went upstairs, Carmine sat at the kitchen table where a lone glass of water waited beside an uneaten biscotti. He didn't touch either, wondering if the ghost of his mother were watching. He pictured Cecilia with her tired grin and chipped nail polish, and heard the laugh that bubbled even when she was bone-weary. Her absence was a cavern, a black hole. No rules or lectures could fill it. Maybe she'd found peace. Maybe not.

He thought of going upstairs, but even sleep seemed pointless. He sat at the kitchen table until dawn, thinking and fighting the hot tears that threatened to fall from his eyes.

∞ ∞ ∞

Carmine stood outside Lafayette High School the next morning in his hoodie, the remnants of spray paint still under his fingernails. But when the bell rang, he turned and walked the other way. He wasn't going back. At this point, school had become almost optional anyway. He would wander in two days a week, maybe three, attending just often enough to avoid truancy charges. His grades had tanked, and he'd started hanging out with an older crowd—guys with switchblades slipped into their socks and cigarettes always tucked behind their ears.

One of them, Louie, had a rusted-out Camaro with a busted tailpipe that roared like a beast. Carmine rode shotgun most nights, windows down, music blasting as they tore through Brooklyn looking for trouble.

"You ever think about what you wanna do with your life?" Louie asked once. They were parked in front of the boardwalk at Brighton Beach with the ocean breeze whipping through the car.

Carmine flicked his cigarette into the wind. "No."

By Friday, the school guidance counselor had left three messages on his family's answering machine. Carmine erased them all before anyone could hear them.

On Monday, Concetta sat at the kitchen table with a folded letter from the school district. Her eyes scanned the paragraph twice. Her knuckles trembled. She waited until Leo came home to say it aloud.

"He's dropped out," she said simply.

Leo looked up from the mail pile. "They called?"

"They wrote. Said he hasn't attended since the Friday before last."

Leo nodded once, as if he already knew the news. "I'll talk to him."

"You'll talk," she said. "And then what? He won't listen."

"He might," replied Leo, never wanting to give up.

Concetta lifted her chin. "He doesn't even hear us, Leo. It's like he walks around with cotton stuffed in his ears and bricks in his shoes."

Leo shrugged. He knew Carmine was upstairs, door closed, music leaking into the hallway. Low, moody guitar riffs came from his door, the kind of music Cecilia used to play when she folded laundry.

That night, Concetta made cavatelli with sausage. Carmine came down only when Leo called him for dinner. The table was silent until Concetta spoke. "I got a letter today."

Carmine stabbed a sausage link, keeping his eyes on the plate. "Okay," he said.

"From the school," continued Concetta.

"Yeah?" muttered Carmine.

Leo wiped his mouth and looked across the table. "You want to tell us what you're thinking, Carmine?"

"I'm not," Carmine said flatly.

"Not thinking?" asked Leo.

"Not going back," Carmine said.

Concetta gasped. "Why?"

Carmine chewed slowly and then took a sip of cola. "What's the point?"

"The point is your future," she said, her voice rising.

"My future's what? College?" Carmine said, half laughing. "A desk job? That's not me."

Leo leaned forward. "You're sixteen."

Carmine dropped his fork. "I'm sixteen and drowning. School doesn't teach you how to breathe underwater."

"That's nonsense," Concetta snapped. "School gives you a ladder."

Carmine looked her in the eye. "No, it gives you stairs. But I'm still at the basement level."

Concetta's hand gripped her glass. "You think this pain makes you special? We all lost Cecilia. But quitting won't resurrect her."

Leo's voice came low and firm. "Enough!"

Carmine stood, his chair scraping hard against the tile floor. "You wanted honesty. There it is." His footsteps thundered up the stairs.

Concetta stared at his abandoned glass of soda. "She'd be gutted," she said. "She wanted more for him."

Leo reached across the table and covered her hand. "She wanted him to do better than just survive."

Carmine didn't sleep. He lay on his bed until dawn, his Walkman playing the music that was supposed to drown out his life.

Two days later, Linda walked through the front door, returning from a short trip with her new fiancé and her usual whirlwind of perfume and bright scarves.

"Geez, why is it so quiet in here?" she said as she stepped into the kitchen. "What happened?" Concetta went to the kitchen drawer, retrieved the letter, and handed it to her. Linda read it, her eyebrows lifted but not surprised.

"He dropped out?" she said, glancing toward the stairs. "Well, that doesn't surprise me in the least."

"Don't say that," Concetta said.

"He's grieving, he's angry, and he doesn't trust the world," said Linda.

"Do you think dropping out will help him? I don't," replied Concetta.

Linda sat down at the table. "I think he needs something to tether him, something that maybe we can't give him." She washed her hands and began helping her mother with lunch.

It was just before dinner when Leo came in from the garage with an old photo frame he'd been fixing. Linda turned toward him.

"I called Anthony and told him what happened," Linda began. "He said maybe Carmine could work part-time at the restaurant. Dishwasher, maybe prep."

"You think Carmine's gonna go for that?" Leo asked.

"Maybe." Linda paused and then her whole body seemed to brighten. "Oh, and Anthony and I are thinking about this summer for the wedding. Nothing big."

"Good," Leo said before returning his attention back to the frame.

Carmine, barefoot and with his hoodie loose, had come halfway down the stairs. "You're marrying Anthony this summer?"

"You heard?" Linda asked.

He nodded, rolling his eyes.

"He's steady," she said in response to his eye roll. "Sweet. Not flashy."

"Sounds boring," Carmine muttered.

Linda approached him slowly. "Boring keeps you alive."

Carmine's eyes narrowed. "You think I'm gonna die?"

"I think you're trying not to live," she said.

Carmine turned away. "Tell Anthony thanks, but I'm not scrubbing dishes."

Linda didn't fight it. "Then keep drowning," she said quietly. "Or find your own rescue ladder."

∞ ∞ ∞

Needing some air, Carmine climbed out his bedroom window just after 1:00 in the morning. The sky hung heavily over Brooklyn, lit by half-broken neon lights and the glow of apartment windows stacked like puzzle pieces. The roof had always been off-limits. Papa said the shingles were unstable, and Nonna said he would break his neck.

Carmine settled near the edge, his Walkman pressed to his chest like it might keep him from falling. Below, a solitary car drove on the asphalt. Somewhere, a siren wailed like a distant violin. Carmine slipped on his headphones but didn't play any music. He just needed to muffle the sounds of the city.

Brooklyn pulsed below, swarming with nighttime tension. But from up there, the chaos softened, and Carmine relaxed a little. He sat with his legs dangling over the roof's edge, his hands shoved into the pockets of his hoodie. No music. Just wind and distant sirens.

The skyline twinkled like a tired constellation. Low buildings, rusty water towers, and bridges threaded across the black space. Manhattan glittered in the distance, sharp and orderly like it didn't bleed. He didn't speak. Didn't cry. Just stared out, and the skyline stared back.

A breeze tugged at his sleeves. It carried faint aromas—stale garlic left over from someone's dinner, weed from a nearby stoop, something floral and familiar. Rosewater maybe. Concetta's lotion. Or his mother's cream from back when she had Sunday skin-care rituals.

He closed his eyes and tried to imagine Cecilia's voice. Not the singsong one. The tired one, the raspy one from worry and too many cigarettes. "You got fire in you," she used to say. "But you gotta learn where to aim it." Carmine wondered how he was supposed to aim for something he couldn't see.

Below, a car alarm chirped once and stopped. Carmine's gaze fell to the gutters lining the edge of the house, packed with dead leaves and rainwater. He thought about jumping—not to die but just to feel the fall. The ground wasn't far enough down to matter.

He breathed into the air: "I didn't mean to become this."

Far off, the Verrazzano Bridge, distant and dreamlike, glowed faintly. He imagined walking it in the middle of the night. No destination. No explanation. Just step after step until the ache quieted.

He leaned back on his elbows, breathing in the damp air. The city was louder when you tried to escape it. His mind drifted to Anthony's dishwasher job offer. He was a steady guy, Aunt Linda had said. Not flashy. Carmine felt himself bristle just thinking about it—"steady" wasn't his currency.

The stars above, sparse and barely winning against the city lights, blinked faintly. "You would've made me finish school," he whispered. "You would've fought harder than Papa."

His chest tightened. He could feel his mother in the space between his breaths, in the gaps no one else could feel. The silence stretched.

Eventually, Carmine stood. He walked to the chimney and tapped a brick once. No reason. He stayed outside for ten more minutes, letting the skyline remind him of everything he wasn't yet ready to become.

CHAPTER 6:

The Sunshine State (1986)

The bus hissed behind them, steam curling up like a warning. Carmine kept his hoodie zipped up and his duffel slung low, his fingers twitching around the strap.

Concetta wrung her hands. "You have enough socks?"

Carmine nodded, his eyes tracing the cracks in the cement. "Aunt Linda said she'd take me shopping if I need anything."

Leo squinted at the bus, his jaw locked. "Florida's heat will mess with your head, but it will do you some good."

"Better than Brooklyn's cold," Carmine said.

Concetta stepped in, touching his arm. "You call. Even just once a week. I don't care if it's just to say you're alive."

"I will," he murmured. A long pause followed before Carmine shifted his weight. "I can come back if it doesn't work out."

"No," Leo said quickly. "Don't look back. Looking back is how people trip."

"Will you miss me?" Carmine asked. It came out softer than he'd intended.

Leo stared at him for a long moment. "Your grandmother will." Concetta nodded, agreeing. "Your nonna loves you more than the rosary beads she clutches."

"I know," Carmine said.

"We'll visit when Linda's twins are baptized," Concetta added. "And send us pictures. I want to see your smile down there."

"I will. I'll ask Aunt Linda to get me a Polaroid camera," he replied. Then he looked at Leo. "Any last advice?"

Leo leaned in. "Fix your posture. Stop flinching. And don't fall for the first girl who says you have sad eyes."

Carmine almost laughed. "Ha, like that's gonna happen."

A horn blasted once from the bus. Carmine reached out—awkward, unsteady—and hugged Concetta first. She clung, murmuring a prayer against his shoulder. Leo had to practically pull his wife out of the embrace.

Leo clasped Carmine's hand. Firm. Quick. "Go set your new course. You're eighteen now, a legal adult. You need to make good choices."

Carmine stepped back, his breathing tight. "Love you," he said. "And I'm sorry for everything I've put you through."

They didn't say anything back—not out of coldness but habit. Love in their house had always been folded into food, advice, and silence.

Carmine climbed the bus steps, duffel thudding behind him, and then turned once. He found a seat near the back. Through the window, he saw Concetta waving with both hands. Leo didn't wave, but his eyes didn't leave his grandson until the bus pulled away.

Carmine hadn't said goodbye to his buddies in Brooklyn. Not to Paulie, his oldest friend. Not to Louie. Not to the guys who hung around McDonald Avenue like phantoms in ribbed tank tops. Carmine just had to leave.

∞ ∞ ∞

The windows of the bus were smeared with fingerprints and stories Carmine didn't care to know. It rumbled past flat stretches of the southern highway. The sun was thicker here, fat and unforgiving as it poured in over the cracked vinyl seats. Carmine sat with his forehead pressed to the glass, watching palm trees flick past like scenes from someone else's life.

Aunt Linda's voice was still in his ear: "You're not a bad kid, Carmine," she told him, even when he got in trouble. "You just never had anyone show you how to do things the right way." He knew she meant it, and that was part of the reason he trusted her more than anyone else. She had always been his lifeline, providing him with the strength and stability that his mother, despite her best efforts, could never give.

Aunt Linda had warned him for nearly two years: "You should move down here with us because you're going to wind up dead or in jail if you stay. Leave before Brooklyn buries you, Carmine." So when she sent him a bus ticket to Florida, he packed up—a few T-shirts, jeans, two pairs of shorts, and his gold chain with a cross pendant—ready to leave immediately.

It was near dusk when he stepped off the bus in Fort Lauderdale, the sky blooming in bruised purples and streaks of orange. Aunt Linda was waiting at the curb, waving like she'd won the lottery. She wore a bright floral blouse and pink lipstick that made her grin look younger than it should have. Carmine thought, *She's the healthy, happy version of my mother.*

"You look thin," she said, hugging him hard. "Don't think I won't fatten you up."

Uncle Anthony honked from behind the wheel of his shiny Chrysler. "Carmine!" he shouted, one hand out the window. "You're here. Finally."

In the back, two baby car seats were wedged in, leaving just enough room for Carmine to squeeze between them. The twins, Cassandra and Jennifer, stared at him with matching sets of wide eyes and apple cheeks while teething on identical plastic giraffes.

"They're monsters," Linda said proudly. "But you'll love 'em."

The house was modest: one story, stucco, with a gardenia bush blooming out front and wind chimes that sang whenever the breeze caught them. Linda had prepared the guest room for her nephew, putting fresh sheets on the bed, bringing in an old dresser of Anthony's from his bachelor days and placing a photo of Cecilia on the nightstand. When Carmine first saw his room, he stared at it a little too long.

The first night, they ate spaghetti and meatballs. Linda kept refilling Carmine's plate until he groaned, stuffed. Anthony cracked open cold beers while the babies babbled over cartoons.

"You're staying," Linda said, tapping her nephew's hand. "This is your new life."

"Alright," Carmine said, actually meaning it. The Florida sun felt like it might melt away some of the ice that had built up in his chest over the years.

The next week, Linda lined up a job for him. She handed Carmine a crisp polo shirt and pointed to the barbershop on

Sunrise Boulevard that was tucked between a Cuban market and a liquor store. It smelled of talc and old leather, and the air was filled with the hum of electric shavers. The owner, Mario, had thick glasses and a laugh that lived in his belly.

"You sweep. You watch. You learn," he said, handing Carmine a broom.

Carmine didn't argue. He swept. He watched. He learned.

The barbershop became a ritual. Carmine swept the floor with absolute precision, watching Mario shape lives strand by strand. Clippers hummed like lullabies. Clients—teachers, truck drivers, fathers—came in with the noise of life on their shoulders and left just a little bit lighter. There was something holy about the barbershop, something Carmine could appreciate.

Three weeks in, Mario handed him the clippers.

"You've got still hands," he said. "Let's teach them something."

It wasn't his own talent that kept Carmine coming back but rather the steadiness of the shop—the way time folded into the rhythm of buzzing and snipping. After hours he stayed late, practicing fades on mannequin heads. Linda stopped by with sandwiches. Anthony offered helpful advice. The twins accompanied their parents, giggling each time Carmine dramatically nicked a plastic scalp to amuse them.

By the time he turned twenty, Carmine had regulars. Men asked for him by name. It felt like belonging. Guys came in with problems, and for fifteen minutes, Carmine could distract them, maybe even make them feel a little better. For the first time in his life, he had a knack for something. His new life didn't erase his past, but now, after years of darkness, Carmine could see a future.

∞ ∞ ∞

Marisol arrived like a spark hitting a gas leak. She worked across the strip in a tattoo parlor and wore leather like skin. Her laugh was unfiltered, and her hips moved like she had secrets worth keeping.

They met on a Tuesday when her scooter broke down in front of the barbershop. Carmine offered to take a look. "Fix it, and I'll buy you a beer," she said.

One beer became three, and three became a wild love. Marisol was chaos in eyeliner and ripped jeans. She pulled Carmine onto beaches at midnight, dared him to dance sober in front of strangers, and whispered things to him in Spanish that he didn't understand but felt deep inside.

One afternoon, after a long walk on the beach, they decided to marry. Right then, with sandy shoes and sunburned cheeks, they headed to the county clerk's office. For a moment, it felt like the kind of recklessness that healed.

But Carmine soon learned that passion burns fast. Arguments started over dishes, money, and nights out. Marisol wanted heat and adventure; Carmine wanted sleep. By the time the divorce came, they were ghosts sharing a kitchen. It ended in a sad fizzle—no screaming, no cheating—with a silence heavy enough to smother them both.

In the middle of the divorce proceedings, Marisol left him a note one morning: "We loved the wrong way." By the time the ink was dry on their divorce papers, neither of them could remember what had brought them together in the first place.

Then came Sarah.

She was everything Marisol wasn't—polished, driven, classy. She was precise like syllables clipped from a grammar school primer. Carmine met her at a charity fundraiser that Mario had dragged him to. Her dress looked like old wealth, and her voice sounded like good schools. She was Jewish, raised in Boca Raton, with a dentist father and a mother who—when they were first introduced—paused too long before shaking Carmine's hand. They thought he wasn't good enough for their daughter.

"You work in a barbershop?" Sarah asked during their first dinner together.

Carmine beamed. "I make people feel better when they look in the mirror."

Sarah's eyes softened. "That's poetic. You're not like I expected."

For a time, they balanced—her ambition, his charm. He followed her to book clubs, and he learned to pair wines with seafood. She liked the way he made the ordinary feel big; he liked the way her order calmed him.

They had a son, Nathan. He was born on a Wednesday while spring thunder rattled the windows. Carmine held him, staring into eyes that matched his own, whispering promises he meant.

But by Nathan's fourth birthday, the little cracks in Sarah and Carmine's union had split wide open. Sarah wanted routine. Carmine wanted rhythm. She needed annual plans. He lived week to week. They talked less. Laughed less. The house got too clean.

They split without drama. No custody battle. No lawyers clawing. Just an ending.

"I don't hate you," Sarah said, folding towels the night before he left. "I just need something else."

Carmine nodded, tracing the outline of Nathan's face on a photo.

"I'll always show up for him," he said. And he meant it.

Last came Diane, the storm.

They met in a Miami nightclub—humidity clinging to skin, neon lights spinning like fever dreams. They were both chasing something they couldn't define. She had red lips and a laugh that curved around lies. Carmine was older now, but Diane made him reckless again.

Their love was gasoline and matchsticks. Fights that started over nothing. A relationship built on highs that never lasted and nights that ended in tangled sheets, empty bottles, and dizzy forgiveness.

Diane worked in retail and danced on weekends. She was four years older than Carmine, yet she cried when he didn't call and screamed when he did. Her intensity felt familiar, so Carmine stayed because calm felt like giving up.

They married on a beach at dusk—barefoot, drunk, her mascara already smeared. No one believed it would last.

But something in Diane dug deeper. It wasn't all gasoline and matchsticks.

Diane didn't mind his silences and didn't push when he stared too long at old photos. And on the good nights—when her kids were out for the night or staying with their father—she would curl up against him, peaceful.

One calm night, tucked into the crook of Carmine's arm as he stared at the ceiling, she said, "I think you're still looking for something."

Carmine kissed her shoulder and closed his eyes. She was the storm, but she also calmed the storm, and that was enough to build their love on.

∞ ∞ ∞

The party swelled with warmth. Carmine's extended family sprawled across the backyard. His cousins visiting from up north for the reunion lounged in lawn chairs, chased after toddlers, and balanced plates of ravioli as they ate. The scent of a fresh-baked ricotta cake floated through the screen door, mingling with citronella and sunblock.

Linda's house overflowed with the kind of joy Carmine never quite understood. It wasn't showy or clean; it was loud and forgiving. Music played from speakers stuck into half-closed windows. Jennifer smeared frosting on Cassandra's nose just to annoy her twin. Anthony shouted something about the Yankees over the buzz of the lawnmower next door.

Carmine stood in the corner of the yard, a cigarette between his lips, watching the party like a man in a distant dream. Diane slipped beside him briefly, kissed his cheek, squeezed his hand, and disappeared inside, barefoot and tipsy from sangria.

Carmine took a drag and exhaled slowly. The air in Florida was soft around the edges, and yet something in him remained taut. Something was still missing.

Inside, Diane wandered into the kitchen where Aunt Linda sat at the table nursing both her wine and her memory. Linda's eyes were watery, with her smile cracked open at the edges. Maybe she was a bit drunk. Maybe she was exhausted from the party. Whatever it was, she didn't look quite herself.

"I love when the house is like this," Linda murmured, swirling the white wine in her glass. "So full of life. It's how it should've been . . . years ago."

Diane poured herself a splash of red, hesitating. She could feel it—a shift in the air, something waiting to be said.

Linda looked up at Diane, eyes glistening. "You love Carmine, don't you?"

Diane nodded, almost surprised by how easily the answer came. "I do."

Diane's children, Melissa and Sam, stuck their heads into the kitchen. "Mom, come back to the party," Melissa said. Melissa had just finished her first year in college and wore a pink University of Florida tank top.

Diane hesitated, seeing Aunt Linda's expression. "I'll be out in just a minute, honey. Go save me a hot dog."

"Okay, Mom, but if you're in here too long, I might eat it," teased Sam. He was going to be a senior when high school started in the fall, and his appetite was ravenous.

Linda watched as the kids moved back into the yard and then reached out and took Diane's hand with unexpected force, trembling. "I've kept a secret," she whispered, "for a long time."

Diane leaned in. "What kind of secret?"

Linda glanced at the door and then over her shoulder as if worried that her confession could be stolen by the noise outside.

"Carmine has a sister," she said in the lowest hush she could manage.

Diane blinked, uncertain she'd heard right. "A sister?"

"She was born before him. Your mother-in-law—Cecilia—had a baby girl before she was married. She gave her up for adoption. The family made her do it."

Diane's face froze in shock.

"I swore I'd never tell," continued Linda. "But it's killing me."

"Does he know?" asked Diane.

Linda's voice cracked. "No. And you can't say anything to him. I promised my sister I wouldn't tell a soul."

That night, lying beside Carmine under the low hum of the bedroom fan, Diane stared at the ceiling. Carmine snored lightly, one arm flung across his stomach, fingers twitching like he was reaching for something.

Diane's mind raced. *He has a sister* echoed again and again in her mind.

It couldn't be. And yet it made perfect sense. She thought back to the photos Carmine sometimes stared at and the stories he half-told, the ones he never finished. She noticed the way he sometimes walked like something was following him, the emptiness she could never fill for him.

For days afterward, Diane watched her husband differently. Every mention of his mother felt louder. Every pause was a plea.

She waited weeks until the secret grew too heavy.

It was a quiet Sunday, thick with Florida heat. Melissa had just headed back to college the day before, and Sam was out with friends. Carmine was in the garage, tinkering with his clippers while a baseball game crackled on the radio.

Diane stood in the doorway, arms crossed. "I need to tell you something," she said, her voice quivering.

He looked up, sensing the tension instantly. "What's wrong?"

"It's about your mom—and Aunt Linda," Diane said.

He set the clippers down and wiped his hands. "Okay."

She almost faltered. "You have a sister. A full biological sister. Aunt Linda told me at the reunion."

Carmine didn't move. Couldn't move.

"She was born before you, before your parents were married. Your mom gave her up. The family didn't let her keep the baby. Linda said they all kept it secret like it never happened." Diane hesitated, not sure she should go on. "And I think it's the thing you've been feeling all this time, that emptiness."

Carmine stood slowly and started pacing. "She told you this? At the party? And you sat on it all summer?"

Diane nodded. "I'm sorry. She begged me not to tell you. I didn't know if I should. But I—I couldn't carry it anymore. You deserve to know."

Carmine was stone-still. Then he said almost softly, "I knew something was missing."

Diane nodded, tears blurring her vision. "You weren't crazy."

Carmine didn't say anything more. He turned away from his wife, fists tight at his sides. After several long moments, he got into the car without a word.

The short drive did little to temper Carmine's anger and even less to ease his shock.

Aunt Linda opened the door before he rang the doorbell. Her smile fell the moment she saw him.

"You told *her*?" Carmine asked.

Linda nodded.

"Why not me? Why didn't you tell *me*?"

"Because I promised your mother I wouldn't," Aunt Linda replied. "She was so afraid, ashamed about giving your sister up. She made me swear. I was so young, Carmine. Scared." She moved to take Carmine's hand, but he pulled away. "The family was embarrassed. They thought it was better this way. But it wasn't better. It was cruel."

Carmine pushed into the house. Inside, the living room held its breath. Through the slats of the blinds, the afternoon light striped the floor.

"She was eighteen," Linda continued. "It was a private adoption. The baby was born March 30th, 1967, at Victory Memorial in Brooklyn. I was the one who handed her over to the social worker. Her name—what Cecilia and I called her between us—was Carol Ann."

"Continue," Carmine said firmly. It wasn't a request.

"She was beautiful. Looked like us—your mom and me. Big brown eyes. Cecilia never forgave herself."

Carmine's words came slowly. "Do you know where she went? Who adopted her?"

"No. Only that it was a nice couple from the neighborhood, someone our lawyer trusted. That's all we were told."

Carmine sank into the couch, chest tight.

"Your mother kept that secret until the day she died," Linda added. "It ate at her. It's the reason she was . . . how she was."

Carmine stared at the photo of Cecilia on the mantle for a long while. "I need to find my sister," he said finally. "I have to."

Linda reached for his hand. He didn't pull away this time. "I'm so sorry, honey. I hope you can forgive me. Maybe now I can make this right for everyone." She pushed back his hair and kissed him on the forehead like she did when he was little. "I promise, as long as I'm breathing, I will help you. I swear."

CHAPTER 7:

DAYBREAK AND A BAGEL (1991)

Bensonhurst was just beginning to forget the night, the sky unsure if it wanted to turn blue or gray as Stephanie stepped out of the cab. A light wind tugged at her hair, and she wrapped her leather jacket tighter around her as she turned toward the glowing red neon sign of Bagel Den.

"Ugh! I'm starving," she muttered to herself, rubbing her stomach. The bell over the door let out a weary jingle as she pushed inside, her heels clacking against the speckled linoleum.

Stephanie's cousin Maria had bailed, of course—too drunk, too tired, or maybe too hung up on that guy from the dance floor to care about breakfast. Normally the two of them, plus a few friends, would all pile into the Vegas Diner on 86th Street after a night of clubbing in Bay Ridge, but tonight everyone had disappeared like cigarette smoke in the cold.

Stephanie's breath fogged the glass as she stood in front of the refrigerated drinks, her black, sequined top shimmering faintly, her eyes smudged with day-old mascara. Catching her reflection in the glass, she thought, *Oh, wow! I look like a train wreck after last night. I hope I don't run into anyone I know.*

The smell of fresh bagels and just-brewed coffee enveloped her like a blanket. A few old men sat near the back, muttering over newspapers and buttered rolls. Other than that, the place was empty, save for the man behind the counter in a wrinkled Yankees cap.

As the man wiped down the steel prep table, Stephanie squinted under the fluorescent lights. Something about him looked familiar, but she couldn't place it. She tried not to stare.

He turned, saw her, and froze mid-wipe. "Stephanie Pellegrino?" His voice was surprised but warm, as if he'd just stumbled into a pleasant memory.

She cocked her head in surprise. "Yeah?"

"From Saint Finbar, right? The Catholic grammar school?" He wiped his hands on the rag he was holding. "You lived on Bay 22nd Street, a few houses from the corner. It's me—Matthew DeRosa. I was two grades ahead of you."

Stephanie's eyes widened. "Oh, my goodness. Matthew?" She took a step closer, studying him. He was built broader than she expected, and instead of being short and slight like she remembered, he was tall. His jet-black hair was shorter now, but that boyish grin that produced the cutest dimples hadn't gone anywhere. He was handsome. Very handsome.

"You lived just around the corner near Benson Avenue. You wore that awful plaid tie, right?" She laughed a little.

"And braces. Don't forget the braces," he said, half joking. "I used to see you at recess jumping double Dutch near the fence." Matthew's grin widened. "You were the prettiest girl in the neighborhood. I had the biggest crush on you."

Stephanie felt her face heat up beneath the layer of club makeup. The compliment hovered—unexpected, unbidden—and landed somewhere soft. She looked at him now. He definitely wasn't a boy anymore. She laughed, brushing a strand of hair behind her ear. "Prettiest girl? Get out of here."

"I remember you never gave me a second look," Matthew said, grinning. "But I swear, I told myself if I ever ran into Stephanie Pellegrino again, I'd ask her out. So . . ." He pointed at the counter with mock seriousness. "Here you are."

She raised an eyebrow. "And what? You're gonna ask me out over an everything bagel?"

"Depends," he said, stepping around the counter. "Do you want cream cheese or butter?"

Stephanie hesitated. Cousin Maria's voice echoed in her mind: *Get a bacon, egg, and cheese, and get back into a cab—don't go flirting with some bagel boy.*

She pushed the voice down. She giggled and then folded her arms across her chest. "What are you doing working here? I thought you were going to be a teacher or something."

"I own a small specialty printing company. I knew I didn't want to work for someone else. And I figured that life doesn't wait, so why should I? This job is just a side gig for early cash flow and early coffee. And it keeps me humble."

Stephanie nodded. "Humble bagel man. I like it."

"Let me make you something," he said, already reaching for the tongs.

She watched him as he worked, his forearms strong, his movement efficient and confident. When he finished, he handed her a bacon, egg, and cheese on a sesame bagel.

"Why don't you sit?" he said, gesturing to the row of seats at the counter. "You look like you've been up all night."

"I have," she admitted, sliding onto a stool. "Club Mirage. Dancing since midnight."

Matthew leaned in, resting his elbows on the Formica. "Still got moves?"

"Oh, please. I wore these heels for four hours—that's the real miracle." They both laughed.

"And this—here, now, in this bagel place—is this your moment to ask me out?" Stephanie asked cheekily.

"Would you let me cook you dinner?"

"What kind of dinner?" she asked, smirking just a bit.

"Chicken milanese. Penne vodka. Best in Brooklyn. I swear," he answered.

She looked at him—really looked at him—and saw something solid, something warm, not the glimmer of the club light, not the noise of the past few years, not the longing emptiness that followed her everywhere. It was something real, almost tangible. "Okay, bagel boy. You've got my attention."

He caught her a cab after she finished her sandwich. The sun was just starting to shine over Bensonhurst.

Matthew called her the next day—and the day after that. They talked for hours about old teachers, neighborhood gossip, how odd it was to grow up so close to each other while being virtual strangers. She liked the way he listened, really listened.

Within weeks, they were inseparable. Stephanie wasn't used to relationships that felt this easy. Dating Matthew was like slipping into a perfectly warm bath after a long, cold day. He was smart and funny, never played games, and never tried to change her. He showed up when he said he would. He brought her flowers just because. And—bonus—his chicken cutlets were breaded by hand, golden and crispy, and his penne vodka had just the right kick of heat.

∞ ∞ ∞

Stephanie's fork glided perfectly through the al dente pasta as she sat across from Matthew in his dim kitchen. The flavors, the textures, and the care the food was prepared with all had her enraptured.

"You weren't bluffing," she said, licking sauce off her thumb. "This is borderline marriage material."

"I'm just saying," he replied with mock seriousness, "there are men who write poetry, and then there are men who sauté. Priorities."

The radio hummed behind them, a late-night Motown station folding into the quiet space. Stephanie's club friends had scattered in recent days, off working shifts or chasing distractions and retreating into their corners of Brooklyn. She hardly noticed though, and she had started mentioning Matthew to the people who mattered most—to Maria, to her mother, to her older neighbor Lidia.

As they ate, Stephanie glanced around the apartment as if it were the first time she was there. Matthew's home was modest but inviting—a Yankees jersey thrown over the couch, a small bookshelf lined with biographies and cookbooks. Nothing felt staged. Nothing was ostentatious. It was all reassuring.

"Let's make a deal," Matthew said. "Every time I make dinner for you, you have to tell me something you've never told anyone."

Stephanie raised an eyebrow. "That's not how meals work."

"Ah," he said, pointing his fork dramatically. "That's how *this* meal works."

Stephanie leaned back, considering. "Okay, let's try it. First one?" He nodded, smiling patiently, encouragingly. "I used to pretend that I had a brother or sister," she began. "Someone to play with. Someone to look after me. Someone who—who would fill this weird space I have inside."

Matthew's expression saddened a touch. "I get that. I can hardly imagine being an only child."

Her voice wavered but didn't falter. "Sometimes I still imagine a sibling, like they're in my peripheral vision but I can't quite see them."

They sat quietly for a moment, the clink of cutlery filling the space that words couldn't. Matthew reached for her hand. His palm was calloused but warm.

Matthew came from a big, boisterous family—two sisters and an older brother—who embraced Stephanie with wide arms and generous hearts. As an only child, Stephanie had never known this kind of chaos, this kind of belonging. She found herself soaking in the noise, the shared memories, the overlapping voices around the table. Their inside jokes became her jokes too. She revered his parents. It was a little like being with her extended family, but Matthew's family was closer, all of them together almost as one. It was the family she'd always imagined but never believed she'd have for herself.

And Stephanie's mother, Angelina, just adored Matthew—his kindness, the way he looked at Stephanie like she was his whole sky. Her daughter had found someone steady, someone good, and some deep part of her relaxed. And Matthew was from a fine family. Angelina knew Jack would have approved tenfold.

The months passed, and Stephanie and Matthew's relationship grew even deeper. Stephanie traded in Friday night clubbing for dinners with Matthew, often at his place. She let her hair grow out at his suggestion, her soft brown curls brushing her shoulders so he could stroke her locks.

Matthew was already cooking when she walked in. In her oversized cardigan, she started unpacking two bags from the Italian deli down the street. The scent of garlic and basil hung in the air, inviting and familiar. The table was set with candles, and a Jerry Vale album played in the background.

The sauce simmered; the veal sizzled. Matthew plated her dish with the kind of concentration reserved for surgeons and romantics.

"Dinner is served," he said with a mock bow. Stephanie inhaled the aroma, kicked off her heels, and sat down. She took a bite of the veal parmesan. Perfect.

She pointed to the candle. "Are we celebrating something?" she asked.

Matthew gazed at her and showed off his dimples. "Maybe," he said.

They ate. They drank wine. They danced in the kitchen.

Just as Stephanie was finishing the last bite of her cannoli, Matthew dropped to one knee.

Stephanie blinked. "What are you doing?"

He pulled a small, leather box from his pocket and opened it. Inside was the most perfect diamond solitaire with a sparkle that was blinding. "Stephanie Pellegrino, I've waited years to know you. And these past six months have been the best of my life. You make me laugh, you keep me grounded, and you're the most beautiful woman I've ever met. I love you. Will you marry me?"

Stephanie's breath caught. Her hands flew to her mouth. "Oh, my! Matthew!" she stammered. "Matthew, oh, my—"

"Is that a yes?" he asked.

She laughed through light-filled eyes. "Of course it's a yes. Can we have a fall wedding?"

∞ ∞ ∞

The October sky was impossibly blue, and the sun was shining brightly on their wedding day—a crisp, golden morning that smelled faintly of fallen leaves and possibility. Stephanie stood in front of the mirror in the sacristy, her white, satin gown hugging her like a second skin. Her hair was pulled back in waves, pinned with tiny pearls. Her makeup was soft and accentuated her cheekbones, but her eyes—glistening and on the verge of tears—betrayed her emotions.

Angelina fussed with her veil. "You look like a porcelain doll, sweetheart."

Stephanie smiled weakly.

Angelina knew her daughter well, knew she was struggling inside. “I know, honey. I know you’re thinking about him.”

“He should be here. I just keep wondering.” Stephanie’s voice wavered. “What would Dad say to me right now?”

Angelina put her hands on her daughter’s shoulders. “He’d say you look breathtaking. And he’d be proud. So proud!”

Uncle Frank, Stephanie’s godfather, arrived just before noon, dressed in a black tux and smelling faintly of cologne. He was the only person who could ever possibly stand in for her father on her special day, and gratefulness washed over Stephanie when she saw him. “You ready, mi bella?” he asked, voice shining with pride.

Stephanie looked at him and then at her mother. “Ready as I’ll ever be.” And with that, Uncle Frank escorted her through the back hallway to the church’s vestibule.

Stephanie greeted her bridesmaids, all dressed in emerald green, and kissed the cheeks of the groomsmen in their matching ties and cummerbunds. The church doors swung open, and the bridal party began walking down the aisle.

Stephanie stepped up, last in line, holding onto Uncle Frank’s arm for dear life. The music played the opening notes of the bridal chorus, and the guests in the pews stood up and turned in unison. A rustle of fabric. A collective heartwarming sigh. Stephanie and her godfather walked down the aisle to the sound of the church organ.

Her heart raced. A tear trickled down her cheek. Her eyes darted around as if she still hoped her father might appear in the flesh, just this once.

As Stephanie reached the altar where Matthew stood—sharp in his tux, eyes brighter than she’d ever seen them—they locked eyes, and she exhaled. Her sadness dissipated as a new joy flooded her. He took her hands and brushed her thumbs with his. No words needed. Just presence and unconditional love. Steady, reliable, unwavering presence—steady, reliable, unwavering love.

∞ ∞ ∞

Being married suited Stephanie. She loved being a wife. Life was good.

After four years of fun and travel, she and Matthew decided it was time to start a family. Just before Halloween, baby Jonathan arrived with his dark eyes and quiet strength. Stephanie knew from the start that he was exceptional. Her son was gentle, perceptive, and layered with complexity. His speech was delayed, and he was sensitive to loud noises. That concerned her a bit, but mostly she chalked it up to his personality. It wasn't until he was three and a half years old that the autism diagnosis came—and it hit Stephanie like a truck. She cried for twenty minutes in the parking lot of the pediatric neurologist's office and then drove home.

The word hung in the air, sterile and clinical, and yet it didn't change how she saw Jonathan. If anything, it deepened her understanding of him. And Matthew never faltered. "We'll figure it out," he said, wrapping his arms around Stephanie. "One day at a time."

Jonathan didn't need fixing. He needed support, understanding, and love. He had that in abundance. Stephanie saw to it. There were speech therapists, occupational therapists, weighted blankets, meltdowns in supermarkets, progress, setbacks, and tiny but miraculous victories. The first time Jonathan said "I love you," Stephanie sank to the floor in happy tears.

A few years later came Gabriella, a firecracker in pigtails. From the moment she could walk, she stomped with purpose. She had Stephanie's eyes, her sass, and none of her insecurities. At four years old, Gabriella demanded to pick out her own clothes and told strangers in the grocery store that her daddy made the best pancakes.

"She's you." Matthew said one night, laughing as Gabriella paraded around in a tutu and rain boots. "The good parts. The passionate parts."

Stephanie couldn't help comparing her two children. Jonathan's babyhood had been quiet, with his gaze wandering and his responses slow. With Gabriella, everything came fast: words, tantrums, laughter. Stephanie was often caught off guard, charmed and unsettled by the vivid contrast.

One afternoon, Gabriella was coloring a sun over a green field covered in flowers while Jonathan stacked his lettered blocks in alphabetical order, reciting each letter with intensity.

Stephanie sat between them on the rug, legs crisscrossed, watching. "I always wanted siblings when I was growing up," she said quietly, more to herself than to her children.

Gabriella barely looked up and said, "I have one. He's weird."

Jonathan paused, tilting his head. "I'm not weird."

Gabriella pointed at his blocks. "You put three Js in a row."

Jonathan went on building calmly. Stephanie stroked his hair. "You're not weird, sweetie. You just see things other people miss."

Jonathan leaned into her touch, and for a moment, the room stilled.

Motherhood kept her busy, yet Stephanie found herself staring at her reflection more often now, not out of vanity but from curiosity. Her features hadn't changed much—same high cheekbones, same thick hair. But motherhood had shifted her gravity. It made her feel both more rooted and more adrift at the same time. The nagging doubts from her childhood never left her, and she wondered about her true origins.

What if I really am adopted? she often thought to herself, the question growing stronger now that she was a mom. *What would that mean for me? What would that mean for my children?* The questions continued to perplex her, and many nights she stared out the window at the sky after Matthew fell asleep beside her. *I have a wonderful life, and I grew up with nothing but love, so why do I still feel this way?*

CHAPTER 8: SEEKING (2003)

Carmine hadn't slept in days, maybe weeks. The nights were long, silent stretches in the glow of his computer monitor, broken only by the scratch of pen against paper when he made notes. Since Diane's words, "You have a sister," had detonated in his chest, nothing felt solid. He'd forgiven Aunt Linda for keeping her secret, but the walls of his life now pulsed with questions.

He moved through the house like a specter. Mugs collected beside the sink, and the coffee inside them was half-drunk and cold. He barely noticed Diane's son, Sam, as he came and went. Notepads littered the kitchen table, all filled with names, dates, and fragments of memory. His sister was out there. He could feel it.

Carmine didn't know her name. He didn't know the shape of her face or the sound of her voice. But he knew she existed, and that was enough to start a search. From the moment he heard the truth, his life had narrowed to a single mission: Find her. Find the missing piece of his soul.

He didn't ease into his search. He dove in head first. The need to know consumed him—mornings, afternoons, long nights that bled into dawns. When Carmine wasn't at work, he was glued to his computer or making calls, scribbling on notepads, and chasing shadows. He barely ate, and sleep evaded him. The thought of his sister filled every quiet moment. Who was she? What had she become? Did she look like him? Did she know she was adopted? Did she ever wonder why?

He registered with every adoption-reunion company he could find. He went to the university for DNA testing and uploaded the results to several genealogy websites, hoping maybe, just maybe, someone out there had done the same. He took out ads in local Brooklyn newspapers and posted messages on message boards.

"Seeking female born on March 30, 1967, at Victory Memorial Hospital, Brooklyn, New York. Italian-American birth parents. A private adoption. You have a brother searching for you."

She had no official name, just the one his mother and Aunt Linda had whispered to each other: Carol Ann. The name became Carmine's anchor.

The first roadblock came almost immediately. Carmine called the New York City Department of Health's vital records office. His voice trembled with urgency as he explained. "My mother gave up a baby for adoption. My older sister. Please. There has to be some way—"

The woman on the phone cut him off gently. "I'm sorry, sir. New York State has closed adoption laws. Those records are sealed unless both parties petition the court. Even then it's rare, especially with private adoptions."

Sealed. The word made Carmine want to punch a wall. How could something so vital—so personal, so necessary—be shut away like it didn't matter? Hidden. Erased like it wasn't his blood, his history, his family.

Carmine stared at the wall after he hung up, his heart pounding. It felt like the world was telling him she didn't exist. But he knew better.

He mailed the paperwork anyway, even though the office told him it wouldn't help. He wrote letters to adoption agencies, Victory Memorial Hospital, even the law office where Aunt Linda vaguely remembered the adoption being processed. Most didn't reply. A few sent form responses. None offered anything solid.

Still, he persisted. He tried everything. He even emailed strangers that he found on the forums.

"Hi. I know this is strange. Were you born on March 30, 1967, in Brooklyn? Were you adopted?"

Most didn't write back. A few wrote back with a polite no. One woman replied kindly to say she wasn't the one he was looking for but that she wished him luck.

Carmine wasn't deterred. He needed more. He turned to his extended family and old friends.

He called everyone—distant cousins in Long Island, old friends of his grandparents, neighbors who still lived in Bensonhurst. Most claimed they didn't know anything. One older cousin paused a little too long and then said in a hushed tone, "I remember your mom being gone for a while. She went to stay with someone upstate. I think there was a baby. There was a rumor. But nobody talked about it back then. People did what they had to do in those days, especially in Italian families."

The words made Carmine's blood boil. Secrets, shame, and silence—that's what had stolen his sister from him. That's what had stolen his mother's peace.

He got a broadband connection so he could stop squabbling with Sam over the phone line always being tied with by his Internet use. With the new, faster connection, he checked the adoption forums even more obsessively. Refresh. Refresh. Refresh.

Diane tried to support him at first. She listened. She sat with him late into the night while he ranted about how unfair it all was. She even helped him organize his notes and make sense of his journal scribbles. She knew the weight he carried, how haunted he'd always been. She hoped that maybe, just maybe, a breakthrough would heal him.

As the months went by, the search devoured him. Carmine stopped sleeping, barely worked, and stopped talking unless it was about his sister. Even Diane began to fade into the background, just like everything else.

It was a Thursday night. Diane stood in the doorway of their bedroom, arms crossed, watching Carmine scribble furiously into a notebook. The TV was on behind him, muted. Nathan was asleep in the spare bedroom.

"You missed dinner again," Diane said. "You're spiraling. You're not eating, you're hardly working, you're—"

"—Do you remember what my mother said before she died?" he interrupted. "Her last words to me were, 'Did you talk to your sister yet?' That wasn't some dying delusion. She wanted me to find her."

"I know. I understand," Diane said, "but I'm afraid you're losing yourself."

Carmine didn't look up. "I'm close. I found a woman born in Brooklyn on the same date. She posted on a reunion site a while back. I messaged her."

Diane stepped into the room. "You said that last week. And the week before."

Carmine's fingers paused on the keyboard. His eyes flicked up to meet hers, wide and intense. "She might be her." His eyes were bloodshot, rimmed with exhaustion.

"And she might not," Diane shot back.

"I can't stop now."

Diane sat on the edge of the bed, her voice low. "Why not? You've stopped everything else."

"What's that supposed to mean?"

"It means your son asked me why you don't come to his games anymore. It means the electric bill is overdue, and we don't have the money to cover it. It means you've barely spoken to either of my kids in weeks. It means I'm tired of eating dinner alone while you chase a ghost."

Carmine flinched. "She's not a ghost."

"She is to us," said Diane.

The silence expanded between them. Diane stood, walked to the door, and then paused. "I miss you," she said, "but I don't know who I'm missing anymore."

On the nights when exhaustion overcame him, Carmine fell asleep with the computer still glowing on the desk across the room, browser tabs open to pages of forum posts and genealogical databases. Other nights he just stared at the ceiling. The dark came not with peace but with the ache of things unresolved.

He remembered the final call from his mother, her voice weak and breaking from cancer. Now that he knew her last words to him weren't morphine-induced babble, they haunted him, echoing in his mind each night. The regret from practically dismissing her, from not pressing her for more information, shattered him.

The new year arrived. Nothing changed. The days became longer as winter ended, but Carmine hardly noticed. In the spring, when Sam graduated and was looking forward to college, Diane forced Carmine to go to the ceremony, but he didn't go to the party afterward.

When the news came that Aunt Linda was sick, Carmine began visiting her every day. Leukemia was ravaging her with a frightening speed. He sat by her bedside and told her updates about the search. "I'm still digging," Carmine told her, gripping her hand. Aunt Linda would croak out a few words of encouragement.

"Do you remember anything else?" he asked her once, desperate. "Anything about the lawyer?"

Aunt Linda's skin was paler than usual that day, and her eyes were sunken, but she still gave her nephew a small smile. She shook her head slowly. "Just that he wore a bowtie. And his office smelled like pipe tobacco."

Carmine chuckled despite himself. "That narrows it down to half of Brooklyn."

Linda's eyes sparkled with amusement. "I'm sorry, honey. I wish I could give you more," she said. "I've thought about that baby every day. And I've prayed for her every night."

"It's okay," he said. "You gave me the most important part—the truth."

A week later, Linda was gone. Carmine felt as if the universe were taking away every lifeline he ever had, one by one.

He didn't cry at the funeral. He just stood there in a black suit that no longer fit properly, staring at the casket being lowered into the earth. With his grandparents long passed, the last living witness to his origin story had vanished. Aunt Linda had been the last thread connecting him to his mother. The grief was unbearable.

He sank deeper. Friends stopped visiting as if they'd all suddenly moved away. Melissa and Sam stopped speaking to him. Diane began sleeping in the guest room. The house became quiet and cold, the way his home used to sometimes feel when he was a boy.

∞ ∞ ∞

The bell above the barbershop door jingled as Carmine rushed in, discombobulated.

Mario stood behind the counter, arms folded, jaw tight. "You're late again," he said.

Carmine tossed his jacket onto the hook nearest his chair. "I had a call with the Department of Health. I couldn't miss it."

Mario stepped from behind the counter. "You've missed three Saturdays this month. You're cutting out early, coming in late. Your chair's empty half the time."

"I'm dealing with something personal," said Carmine.

Mario's voice rose. "We're all dealing with something. You think I don't have problems? But I show up. I work. You used to be solid, Carmine. What happened?"

Carmine's jaw clenched. "I'm trying to find my sister. She was put up for adoption before I was born. And I didn't even know that until recently."

Mario's face softened a little. "I'm sorry. I really am. But this is a business. You don't show up, you don't get paid. And I can't keep covering for you."

"I'll make it up. I swear," promised Carmine.

Mario shook his head. "You're not making it up. You're falling apart."

Carmine stepped closer. "Don't talk to me like I'm some flake."

Mario barked, "I'm talking to you like a man who's watching his shop lose money."

Carmine slammed his hand on the counter. "You think I care about money right now?"

Mario didn't flinch. "You'd better start, because if you don't, you won't have a job."

That night, Carmine sat beside his son, Nathan, on the couch, trying to focus on the program on TV. Even though he was older now, Nathan leaned against his father the way he always had since he was a toddler.

"Are you gonna come to my game tomorrow?" Nathan asked.

Carmine hesitated. "I'll try, buddy."

Nathan looked up. "You always say that."

Carmine swallowed. "I know. I'm sorry."

Nathan turned back to the screen without replying.

Later, when Carmine dropped Nathan off at home, Sarah met him at the door with folded arms and pursed lips.

"You missed the science fair at school the other day," she said.

"I had a lead. I thought—" Carmine began.

"—You always think you've found the last missing piece. But it's never the last. You're chasing someone who might not want to be found, and in the meantime, your son is right here. Waiting."

Carmine looked down. "I'm trying."

Sarah's voice softened, but her eyes stayed sharp. "Try harder. He needs you."

The next night, Diane found her husband asleep at the kitchen table, his head resting on a pile of papers. She covered him with a blanket and then sat across from him, staring. She didn't recognize Carmine anymore. The man she married was warm, funny, and present. This man was hollowed out and consumed by a mission she'd stopped understanding.

She whispered, "Come back to us," but he didn't stir.

Everything got harder. The bills piled up. The fridge was half empty. Carmine continued to skip shifts. He missed Nathan's baseball playoffs and forgot Diane's birthday.

Then one morning, Diane packed a bag.

"I'm going to my sister's for a few days," she said, standing in the doorway with her jacket already on. "If Melissa or Sam comes home this weekend, I'll have them meet me there."

Carmine looked up from his new, secondhand laptop. "What? Why?"

"Because I need space," she said. "Because you've stopped trying to be part of this family."

He stood. "You're leaving me?"

"I'm giving you a chance to choose something other than this obsession." She paused and lowered her voice. "And Nathan's not mine, Carmine. When he's here, I'm the one who spends time with him, not you. I love him, but he's not my responsibility. He's your responsibility. And right now, you're disappearing."

Carmine stepped forward. "I'm trying to find my sister," he said weakly.

"And in the process, you're losing everything else," added Diane. She kissed his cheek, soft and sad, and walked out the door.

He didn't stop her. He didn't ask her to stay. Carmine's mind was ten steps ahead, wondering if he'd missed a post in a reunion chatroom while they'd been talking.

That night, alone in the house, Carmine stood in front of a mirror and stared at himself. Gaunt face. Eyes like hollow wells. Hair unkempt. Uneven stubble on his cheeks and chin. He saw why Diane had left.

∞ ∞ ∞

It was late. Carmine scrolled through the adoption boards, just like he did every night. There were stories of reunions—siblings who had found each other through DNA testing, mothers and daughters reuniting after forty years. Every story brought hope . . . and pain.

He slammed the laptop shut and buried his head in his hands. "Where are you?" he cried softly.

He stood up, grabbed his keys, and walked out the door. He drove with no destination—windows down, music off—with just the hum of the engine and the ache in his chest.

He ended up in front of a house he'd only seen once—his father's. When Carmine first moved to Florida, Aunt Linda had told him she'd heard through the grapevine that James lived in Lake Worth with his third wife and two children. Carmine showed up on James's doorstep one evening, but James didn't want anything to do with him. The man wanted to forget his past life altogether. Carmine wrote him off, knowing that James remained a sorry excuse for a man. He was the man his mother had warned him about.

James lived barely an hour away. Carmine had never forgiven him for the past, but now he was desperate for answers. He arrived just after sunrise. Carmine parked the car and waited a few hours, wondering if he should really approach James again. When he could see through the window that the house was waking up, he marched up to the front door, his heart pounding. He knocked politely.

The door creaked open. James stood there, older and heavier with graying temples and the same cold eyes Carmine remembered from his last visit.

"Carmine? What do you want?" James asked flatly.

"I want to know about my sister. I need answers," said Carmine.

James balked. "What are you talking about?"

"Don't play dumb," Carmine insisted. "You and Mom had a daughter before me. Where is she? Do you even care what happened to her?"

James glanced over his shoulder, stepped outside, and closed the door behind him. "It was a different time," he said, keeping his voice low.

"That's not an answer," Carmine growled. "That's my blood. My sister. I have a right to know."

"I don't have any information for you, Carmine. Cecilia's parents took care of everything back then. It was a lifetime ago." James pointed toward the street. "You need to leave."

Carmine stared at him. "You always were a coward."

James puffed up his chest. "Just go."

Carmine turned to leave but paused when he saw through the front window some family photos on the mantel. There was a smiling wife and children. His father had built a whole new life. A clean slate. A second chance. One he'd never offered Carmine.

Carmine spat on the ground as he reluctantly walked away.

The photos on the mantle burned into his mind as he drove home. The perfect family. The perfect house. The warmth. Everything James had never given to his first son.

The drive home was quick with no traffic, so quick that Carmine wondered how his father could be so far away.

Carmine returned to his laptop. More messages. More emails. More forums. More hints that would probably come to nothing.

Not willing to give up, he opened a fresh notebook.

"Why can't I find you?" he said to the empty page. "Do you even know I exist?"

And then, for the first time in weeks, he let himself cry.

CHAPTER 9:
Turning Tides (2006)

The therapist's office was too still. Carmine could hear the tick of the wall clock, the distant hum of traffic through the sealed windows, and even the faint creaking of the leather when he shifted on the couch. Everything felt padded, like the room was trying to muffle him.

Dr. Levin sat across from him, legs crossed, her pen poised above a legal pad. Her voice was calm, practiced. "You said you're working again?"

"A warehouse job," Carmine said. "Third shift. It's fine. I'm paying the bills, keeping the kids fed."

"It's steady work?" she asked. She clicked the pen she was holding, preparing to take notes.

"Mostly," he responded.

She nodded, scribbling something. Carmine hated it when she made her notes. It made him feel judged, like he'd just said something wrong.

"And Nathan?" she asked. "How are things going with him?"

Carmine's jaw flexed. "I see him every other weekend. We do breakfast, the park, sometimes an arcade. I think he's forgiven me for all the time I missed with him."

"That's good," Dr. Levin said. "How do you feel about that—being forgiven, I mean?"

"He might have forgiven me, but I still feel guilty." Carmine scratched his cheek. "I completely bailed on my son for over two years. I promised I would be a better father to him than mine was to me."

Dr. Levin stayed calm and turned back a page or two in her notes. "Yes, you've told me about your father—or lack of one."

Carmine shrugged. "It's getting better at home now. I provide for Nathan, and Diane keeps my schedule and the house finances tight. Sarah was coming after me for back child support."

"Diane's the one who encouraged you to come to therapy, wasn't she?" Dr. Levin flipped through her notes again.

"Yeah. She gave me an ultimatum," he said. "Either I talk to someone or she would walk."

Dr. Levin didn't react, her face remaining calm and even. "And you chose to talk?"

"I chose not to lose my life," Carmine said.

She let his answer sit for a moment and then asked, "How's the search going? Are you practicing the techniques we talked about?"

Carmine's eyes darted to the corner of the room where a potted plant drooped. "I'm searching, but not like before."

"Define *before*," said Dr. Levin.

"Before I started seeing you," Carmine responded, "it was constant, continual. I'd stay up all night combing forums, emailing strangers, chasing leads. I barely left the computer—or the house. I lost two jobs. I completely forgot to pick up Nathan for the weekend once, and I missed a lot of his school events. I was neglecting Diane and her kids, and she moved out on me for a while once. She went to stay at her sister's for a little while, but she came back home."

"That was obsessive-compulsive behavior," Dr. Levin said.

"I know. You've told me."

"And now?" she asked, uncrossing and recrossing her legs.

"I'm doing what we talked about. Now I check the boards and chatrooms at designated times—during breaks at work, once in the morning, and once before bed. I've got Google alerts set up that do a lot of the work for me. I keep it contained."

Dr. Levin tilted her head. "Do you feel contained?"

He gave a dry laugh. "I'm not screaming at random strangers in parking lots, if that's what you mean."

"That's not what I mean," she said, a frown in her voice.

Carmine leaned back, his arms crossed. "I'm functioning. I work. I sleep. I eat. I see my kid. I'm not spiraling anymore."

"But you're still searching," Dr. Levin said.

"Of course," Carmine said firmly. "How could I not?"

Dr. Levin waited a moment. "Can I ask something?"

"You're the one with the notepad," said Carmine.

"What drives the search now?" Dr. Levin continued. "It's been three years."

Carmine stared at the ceiling as if something interesting were plastered there. "I didn't know she existed, not until three years ago, as you said. There was one conversation at a family party, and all of a sudden, I had a sister, a whole person out there. How can that not drive me?"

"But you haven't found her," said Dr. Levin.

Carmine responded. "No. All I have to go on are loose facts, a little girl born before me. All I have are maybes."

Dr. Levin's pen paused. "You're searching for someone you've never seen."

"I'm searching for someone who's mine," he said firmly. "Blood. Family. That doesn't go away just because I didn't know."

She nodded. "Do you feel like you missed something?"

"I feel like I was robbed," Carmine said, dejected.

"That must be a hard feeling to carry," said Dr. Levin gently. "Why don't you tell me more?"

"I was robbed of knowing her. Of being there. Of . . . I don't know. Of mattering," he said.

Dr. Levin's gaze softened. "You're trying to matter to someone you've never met."

Carmine's throat tightened. "Did you ever feel like there was a piece of you missing, but you didn't even know it was gone until someone pointed it out? Confirmed it?"

She sat patiently, waiting for Carmine to finish the thought.

"That's what it feels like," Carmine continued. "It's like I'm walking around with a hole in me."

Dr. Levin scribbled something and then looked up. "And Diane?"

"She's so tired of all this, and so are her kids. She still thinks I'm obsessed."

"Are you?" Dr. Levin asked. "Even with the progress we've made these last six months?"

Carmine hesitated. "I'm careful now. I keep it in a box. The urge to know never goes away, but I keep it in a box."

"Does the box stay closed when you're with Diane?" asked Dr. Levin.

"I try. I took her out to dinner the other night, and we almost had a nice time."

"That's very good, Carmine," Dr. Levin said brightly, making a note. "Now what about when you're with Nathan? Still contained?"

"For the most part," Carmine said. "I try not to talk about it with him, but sometimes it's tough. He's old enough now to understand these things. He has an aunt somewhere out there, and he should know that."

"And what about when you're with your stepkids?"

"I don't talk to them about it," Carmine replied. "I don't talk to them about much. They can't stand me, and that's not going away anytime soon."

"Maybe we can talk next week about improving those relationships."

Carmine slouched in response. Dr. Levin didn't press the point further. She let the silence between them fill the room.

"I'm not crazy," Carmine said finally. "I just need to know."

Dr. Levin nodded. "No, you're not crazy, though that's not a word I like to use in here. You have a disorder, an imbalance of sorts, though it is getting better." She paused, scribbling again. "So what would knowing give you?"

Carmine sat up straighter. "Proof. Proof that she's real, that I'm not chasing an imaginary person."

Dr. Levin nodded. "That's a powerful need."

Carmine looked away. "It's exhausting." He could feel his need, tight and heavy, suddenly pressing against his ribs. He shifted in his seat. Nervous. Agitated.

Noticing the change in his demeanor, Dr. Levin said, "Are you feeling anxious, Carmine?"

"A little," he replied, his eyes shifting back and forth.

"Do the breathing exercise we talked about. Take your time. I'll wait."

Carmine inhaled for three seconds, exhaled for four, and then repeated it twice. Each time he felt his breath flowing into his lungs, stretching his tight back muscles, filling him up. He exhaled his breaths slowly, pretending he was blowing his anxiety away.

"Did that help?" Dr. Levin asked a moment after the last exhale.

"A little," Carmine repeated.

"I have another question for you, if you're ready." Carmine nodded, and she continued. "When Diane told you the news—told you she'd talked to your aunt—how did that make you feel?

"Like I'd been lied to my whole life," he said, raising his voice slightly.

"By your mother?" she asked.

"By everyone," said Carmine.

"Did you ever confront her? Your mother?"

Carmine looked her straight in the eye. "She's dead."

Dr. Levin paused. "I'm sorry. I didn't know. We should talk about that in another session."

Carmine nodded, his eyes fixed on the floor. "I keep thinking that if I'd known sooner, maybe I could've found my sister a long time ago. Maybe I could've stopped us both from feeling abandoned."

"But you don't know if she feels that way," said Dr. Levin. "She may know nothing about this at all."

"I know how I felt, how I still feel," Carmine retorted.

Dr. Levin scribbled something again. "Do you think this search is about her? Or about you?"

Carmine's jaw clenched. "It's about both."

She didn't challenge him. She just waited for him to continue.

"I just want to know if she's okay," he said, "if she's alive, if she's ever wondered."

Dr. Levin leaned back. "And if she didn't?"

He swallowed. "Then I'll stop. I won't contact her again."

"Are you sure you could let it go?" Dr. Levin asked. The click of her pen retracting had an odd finality to it.

Carmine didn't answer.

∞ ∞ ∞

Out on the back patio, Carmine lit another cigarette with the butt of the last, the glow briefly illuminating the hollows beneath his eyes. The overhead light cast a yellow glow across the stone pavers. He didn't notice the moths fluttering around it or the way the damp night air clung to his skin. He was somewhere else—somewhere suspended between what was and what must be.

Inside, Diane stood at the kitchen sink, watching him through the window. Her fingers gripped the edge of the counter, knuckles white. Her frustration was a living thing—tight in her chest, coiled and pulsing like a muscle that refused to unclench. She was in desperate need of another Xanax.

She could see Carmine was trying. He'd been going to therapy faithfully for well over a year. She appreciated his progress, appreciated the attention he tried to give her, and was thankful for the effort he was making with her kids. But still, some part of her husband was always somewhere else—somewhere she couldn't reach. Every dead end was another heartbreak. Each one was another thread that slipped through Carmine's hands, leaving him more tangled and hurt inside than before.

In a last-ditch effort to pull him back to life—and maybe to salvage their marriage—Diane, still gripping the counter, resolved to do something she knew Carmine wouldn't approve of. But she had to try, and if it didn't work, he never needed to know.

The next morning, a rainy Thursday, she made a phone call to a professional genealogist she had found on the Internet. The woman on the other end of the line had a calm, steady voice. "Lisa Goldman," she said into the phone. "Genealogical investigations, reunions, and heir searches. What can I help you with?"

Diane swallowed hard. "I'm looking for someone, my husband's sister. He doesn't know her name, but he knows her birth date and place of birth."

A pause came over the line. "Okay," Lisa said after a moment. "Tell me everything."

They spoke for nearly an hour. Diane told her everything she knew—dates, locations, names, even the few bits Aunt Linda had remembered.

"He's been searching for years," Diane said, twisting the cord of the old wired phone around her finger. "But he's lost himself in it."

"I've spent my career reuniting families," Lisa said when Diane was done. Her voice was kind, soft-spoken yet confident.

"Do you think you can help?" Diane asked at last.

"These things take time," Lisa began, "and I can't make any promises. But I can tell you that I've had good luck with cases like this."

Diane hung up, her heart pounding, her head spinning. She hadn't told Carmine that she found the genealogist. She hadn't asked for his input or his feelings. That wasn't usually how their marriage worked. Yet she had made the call, paid the fee, and was now hoping for a miracle.

A few days passed. Diane desperately wished this was the thing that would bring her husband back to her.

The following Monday, while she was folding laundry in the bedroom, the phone rang.

"I found her," Lisa said.

Diane's heart nearly stopped. Lisa's words were calm, but Diane heard the excitement in her voice.

"Are you sure?" asked Diane cautiously.

"I'm ninety-five percent sure," Lisa replied. "Her name is Stephanie Pellegrino DeRosa. Born March 30, 1967. Victory Memorial Hospital. It was a private adoption arranged through an attorney connected to the Pellegrino family. Everything lines up."

Diane sat down on the edge of the bed and tried to remain composed. Joy crept onto her face. Carmine could come back to her now. Her husband could have peace.

"Stephanie lives in New Jersey now," Lisa continued. "She's married with two children. We have to figure out how you want to proceed from here. I think it would be best if I contacted her first."

Diane hung up the phone and stared at her reflection in the dresser mirror. This was the moment Carmine had been waiting for, the moment that could bring normal—and maybe even happiness—back into their lives. It was the moment when he could meet his sister and put the last four years to rest. Diane felt like she was in shock.

Diane waited until she heard Carmine come in later that evening. She gave herself a few moments before going downstairs, bracing herself for—she didn't know what. When she was ready, she found him outside, chain-smoking again on the back patio.

"Carmine," she said quietly. "We have to talk."

He glanced at her, eyes bloodshot. "What?" he replied. "You know I'm doing my best. Putting the work in. Keeping to the schedule. Engaging with the kids when they're home from school."

"No, it's not that," Diane replied.

Carmine put his cigarette out in the over-full ashtray on the patio table. "Then what is it?"

"I found her."

He blinked as if he hadn't heard her. "What?"

"I hired someone," she said, her voice trembling. "A genealogist. A professional. I know you said you had to do this yourself, but I called her anyway. And she found your sister."

Carmine stared at her, his expression unreadable. Diane couldn't tell if he was about to cry, scream, or laugh.

"You—you found her?" he said, his voice hushed in disbelief.

Diane nodded. "Her name is Stephanie Pellegrino DeRosa. She's real, and she's alive."

Carmine sank onto the step that led up to the glass sliding doors and took off his baseball cap, running his fingers through his hair. His hands were shaking.

Diane handed him a scrap of paper. On it were Stephanie's name, birth date, and the city where she lived.

Carmine held the scrap like it was a sacred artifact. For a long time, he didn't move or say anything.

"Why?" he said at last.

"Because I love you," she said simply. "And you were vanishing."

Finally, he looked up at Diane. "Thank you."

Diane nodded, tears in her eyes. "I just want you to be okay."

He stood and hugged her—really hugged her—for the first time in months. Then he disappeared into the house.

He sat on the edge of the bed for what felt like hours, staring at the piece of paper in his hands as if it were a loaded gun. His heart thundered in his chest. He whispered his sister's real name out loud. "Stephanie."

Questions swirled in Carmine's mind. What if she didn't want to talk to him? What if she hated him for showing up in her life? What if she didn't even know she was adopted?

"I've finally found you," he said to the paper. "But now what?"

CHAPTER 10:

Secrets Shattered (2007)

Stephanie was busy unpacking a box of cookware in the kitchen of her new home at the Jersey Shore, the sun streaming through the windows. Outside, her children and husband splashed in the pool. Matthew tossed Gabriella into the air while Jonathan floated on an inflatable raft nearby. Stephanie's mother, Angelina, was sitting on a lounge chair with a glass of iced tea, watching with happiness in her eyes.

Stephanie reflected on their recent move. Her family's happiness was worth all the work, uncertainty, stress, bidding, disappointments, and chaos of the last few months. They had been living in central New Jersey for the last few years, but the home wasn't ideal, and they wanted to be closer to the seaside. Now their new home had it all—three bedrooms, a den, a pool, and an attached in-law suite that was perfect for Angelina. Point Pleasant had good schools for the kids, and it was still close enough to Brooklyn that they could visit family anytime they wanted to. Life felt happy and stable—even beautiful.

Stephanie was halfway through unwrapping a set of plates when the phone rang. She reached for the receiver absentmindedly, not checking the caller ID. "Hello?"

A calm, professional woman came on the line. "Hi, may I please speak with Stephanie Pellegrino?"

Weird, she thought. *Why is someone asking for me by my maiden name?* "This is she."

There was a short pause. "My name is Lisa Goldman. I'm a licensed genealogist and private investigator. I know this may be a bit out of the blue, but I work on behalf of clients who are searching for biological family members."

Stephanie froze in place, one hand still inside the box of plates. She clenched a wad of packing paper.

Lisa continued gently. "Before I say more, I want to ask: Have you ever been told you were adopted?"

The question landed like a rock on Stephanie's chest. Her pulse surged. The room suddenly felt too warm. *This is it! Here it is*, she thought to herself. *My gut was right all along.*

"I . . . I wasn't told," she replied slowly, "but I've always wondered."

Lisa's tone softened. "I understand this might be shocking, but I have reason to believe you were adopted at birth. I'm contacting you on behalf of my client, Carmine Esposito. He's been searching for his full biological sister for several years. Public and private records about you match the limited information he was able to give me." She went on with further details. Stephanie listened as if her words were a lifeline. "Everything lines up!" Lisa finished.

Stephanie sat down hard at the kitchen table. She stared blankly at the wall, her heart thudding in her ears.

"Part of me always knew," she murmured, her voice nearly inaudible. "Victory Memorial Hospital, you said?"

"Yes. Your birth mother's name was Cecilia Russo Esposito. She was eighteen, unwed at the time. The adoption was arranged privately through an attorney connected to a family friend of the Pellegrinos. Your brother, Carmine, was born to the same parents, though they had married at that point."

Stephanie's mind raced. She thought of the questions she'd been asking her mother since she was eight years old—the times she had been told no with too much force. The missing photos. The stories. Being an only child. The excuse that Angelina had been bedridden in the last trimester—that's why no one ever saw her pregnant. The birth certificate with the raised seal that she'd been told was authentic yet never felt quite right.

Stephanie took a deep breath as something inside her clicked into place. *All those years of wondering. I wasn't crazy after all.*

After a moment she said, "What's his story?" her voice thin.

"He grew up in Bensonhurst, Brooklyn, just like you, although he was in another part of the neighborhood. He's had a difficult life, Stephanie, and he's always felt like something was missing. When he found out you existed, he started searching—for four years."

"He lived that close?" asked Stephanie, shocked.

"Yes, but he lives in Florida now. Unfortunately, your birth mother, Cecilia, passed away years ago. He moved south not too long after her death."

"So how did he learn about me?" Stephanie gasped for air, feeling as if the wind had been knocked out of her. "Through our father?"

"No. Carmine has never had a relationship with his—your—father. He learned about you after your mother's death through her twin sister, Linda, who'd kept the secret for decades. He's been searching tirelessly ever since."

"Does he know my name?

"Yes," Lisa said. "But that's all he knows for now." She paused, giving Stephanie a moment. Then she said, "You've both been living parallel lives without each other, and he just wants the chance to know you."

Stephanie rubbed her temple. She glanced out the window again. Matthew was still laughing with the kids. Angelina was still sipping iced tea, completely unaware of the hurricane about to hit.

"So what happens next?" Stephanie asked, hardly believing that there could be next steps.

"That's entirely up to you," Lisa said, empathy in her voice. "Carmine would love to speak with you, but I won't give out your contact information without your permission. Or I can arrange a call through me if that's more comfortable."

Stephanie was quiet for a long time. She closed her eyes, tears slipping down her cheeks.

"Take your time," Lisa said kindly. "There's no pressure. But I do think he's a good man. He's not after money or anything. He's been through a lot, and he just wants to know you."

Stephanie straightened her spine, getting control of herself. "Please. Please let me think about this for a few days. I will call you back. Thank you for contacting me, Lisa."

That night after the kids went to bed, Stephanie—still stunned—told her husband about the phone call.

"Oh, my goodness, Steph. You always said it. For as long as I've known you, you've said you thought you were adopted." After Matthew hugged her, he looked into her eyes. "Are you okay?"

"Yes, I'm okay. I'm just trying to wrap my head around all this. It's so strange. I'm upset, confused, and happy at the same time." She sat down on the antique hope chest at the end of the bed. "But I'm glad I know. I finally know, Matthew. And I think the first thing I need to do is go downstairs and talk to my mother."

Angelina was sitting at the kitchen table, her nightly cup of chamomile tea cradled in her hands. She looked up as Stephanie entered, her expression expectant. Her daughter was never up this late.

Stephanie sat down across from Angelina. "Mom, when were you going to tell me? Probably never? Or maybe I was supposed to find out at your funeral."

"Tell you what, sweetheart?" Her voice was soft, inwardly knowing. "What's going on?"

"I got a phone call today," Stephanie began, "from a genealogist named Lisa."

All the color left Angelina's face. She opened her mouth to say something, but her jaw just hung there, slack.

"She told me the truth," Stephanie said firmly. "She told me about the adoption. About my birth mother. About my brother."

Angelina set the teacup down carefully. Her hands shook slightly.

"I asked you for years," Stephanie said, her voice a harsh, loud whisper. "Since I was a kid. And every time, you lied to me."

"Your father made me promise," Angelina said, her voice cracking. "He was so afraid we'd lose you if you knew the truth. And I . . . I loved you so much. Maybe I was afraid too."

Stephanie's eyes welled. "I've spent my whole life feeling like a stranger in my own skin. Do you have any idea what that's like?"

Angelina reached across the table, but Stephanie pulled her hand away. "We thought if you ever knew, you'd go looking for them." She slumped her chin and gazed down at her nightgown.

Looking up with just her eyes, Angelina continued, her voice lowered. "There were rumors, Stephanie. We heard stories about the kind of life your birth mother lived. After your father died, you were so heartbroken—so lost. I just wanted to protect you, even if it meant keeping something this big from you."

"You think you had your reasons," Stephanie replied harshly, "but I had a right to know."

Tears fell from Angelina's eyes, but she didn't reply.

"What about medically speaking?" Stephanie continued, almost shouting. "I gave every doctor I saw *your* medical history, thinking it was my family's. What about when I was pregnant with the kids?" Stephanie slammed her palm on the table. "You played God with my life!"

Angelina nodded slowly. "You're right. I'm sorry."

"And this brother I never knew grew up in Bensonhurst. What if we'd dated?" Stephanie flung her arms into the air. "What about that? The very thought of it is repulsive."

Angelina's nose wrinkled in disgust. "We, we . . . I don't . . . God wouldn't have let that happen." She breathed in and held it for a moment. "Oh, Lord, help me. I'm sorry, so very sorry."

Stephanie sat there for a long time before she said calmly, "His name is Carmine. And I'm going to talk to him."

With a pained heart, Angelina gazed sadly at the daughter she'd lovingly raised. "Not a day has gone by when you weren't mine."

Stephanie got up from her chair.

Angelina wiped her eyes. "Honey, if you go looking for—"

"—You can't know what I'm feeling, Mom. I'm talking to my brother, and that's the end of it."

∞ ∞ ∞

Stephanie couldn't get her mind to focus on anything—not since she called Lisa back. She completely forgot about parent-teacher night at Jonathan's school, and Matthew had to cover for her. Yesterday afternoon, while unloading groceries with the kids, she almost put a gallon of milk in the pantry, earning her a rebuke from Gabriella. "Mom? Hello? Mom! What are you doing?"

Stephanie had just finished her first cup of morning coffee when the phone rang. She sensed who was calling even before looking at the caller ID. Lisa told her that Carmine was aware that Stephanie had given permission for direct contact.

"I've just sent him your contact details via email," Lisa said. "He's going to call you soon, probably today. I just wanted you to know, to be prepared."

Stephanie didn't know what to say. Pushing back a sudden rush of tears, she managed to eke out a squeak that sounded both positive and thankful.

Lisa continued. "I wish you luck. I hope this is everything you both want and need it to be."

"There's still one thing I don't understand," Stephanie said, gaining control of herself. "I've seen my birth certificate. It has my name and my parents' names on it. It has an embossed state seal and everything."

"I've seen your birth certificate," Lisa said gently. "If you look closely, you'll see that it's stamped with a filing date six months after you were born. That's unusual since most birth certificates are filed within a few days or weeks. The delay was because at that time, the birth mother had six months after the adoption to change her mind. So your birth certificate also served as your name-change certificate."

Stephanie started crying again. "So that does it," she murmured. "That's the last missing piece for me."

"I'm glad I could clear that up for you. And if you need anything else, feel free to reach out to me. Again, I wish you only the best."

"Thank you, Lisa," Stephanie said, now barely controlling her sobs.

Stephanie hung up and stared at the coffee mug in her hand for what seemed like an hour. It was all so real now—and terrifying. She showered, got dressed, sat down, stood up, walked around, and practiced how she would answer the call.

Finally, the phone rang.

"Hello?" Stephanie answered, intentionally not looking at the caller ID.

"Hi. Is this Stephanie?" The voice on the other end of the line made her breath catch.

"Yes."

The caller swallowed hard, audibly. "This is Carmine. I'm your brother."

There was a pause. "You're real." Stephanie's voice trembled.

Carmine let out a broken laugh. "So are you."

"I didn't sleep last night," she said. "I couldn't stop thinking about what you must have been through, about what this means."

"I—I don't know what to say," he stammered.

"You don't have to say much right now if you don't want to," she said. "I'm shaking."

"I've been searching for you for so long," Carmine said, emotion building in his voice. "I didn't know your name or if you even existed for sure. But I felt it. Always."

"I knew something was off since I was a kid," Stephanie replied. "Deep down inside, I knew it—I don't know why. I could never prove anything."

They were quiet for a long, comfortable moment.

"This is like meeting a part of myself I didn't know existed," Stephanie finally said.

"Same," replied Carmine. "You're my sister. This is crazy."

"I have a brother," she gasped. "I can't believe I have a brother. I've never had a sibling."

"Me neither." He laughed softly, though Stephanie could hear the tears filling his eyes. "We're less than a year apart. You know that?" he continued. "You were born in March, on the 30th. I came along the following March, on the 11th. You grew up in Brooklyn, too, right?"

"Yes, I was born there," Stephanie shared. "My family moved to Long Island—Deer Park—for about two and a half years after that, and then we went back to Bensonhurst."

"I was in Bensonhurst until I was eighteen," Carmine said.

They laughed in disbelief when they discovered they'd attended the same high school, just a grade apart. Same borough. Same places. Always within reach of each other.

"That's haunting," Stephanie said. "You were so close—so close to me all that time."

"We probably passed each other many times and never knew it," Carmine replied.

They stayed on the phone for hours, talking about their childhoods, the parents they knew, the secret they never asked for. Stephanie told him about her pink bedroom with the canopy bed, Catholic school, dance lessons, and the Girl Scouts. She told him about her father, Jack, and how his death had shattered her world. She told him about marrying Matthew, becoming a mother to Jonathan and Gabriella, and always carrying a silent ache. She told him about the kids' personalities. She told him how blessed she was, even with the hole inside that she'd secretly carried.

Carmine told her about his opposite life—about their mother Cecilia's chronic depression, her drinking, the rotating cast of men. He told her about the times he comforted her instead of the other way around. He said she died of cancer when he was a teenager.

"I know she loved you," Carmine said. "She was thinking about you, even in her last days. She mentioned you before she passed, but she was too ill to say more. I didn't understand at the time, but now I do. She never forgot you."

Stephanie wiped her eyes. "I wish I could've met her."

He told her about moving to Florida, about Aunt Linda, her family, and her untimely passing. He talked about being a father himself, about how he didn't get to see Nathan as often as he would have liked. He told her about how he'd tried to be a good father even though he'd failed. He shared about his divorces, about what it was like marrying a woman who came with a family of her own.

While they were still on the phone, Carmine emailed her pictures of Cecilia and of himself as a boy and an adult. Stephanie couldn't believe how she resembled her birth mother. Looking at Cecilia was like looking in a mirror, and her heart flooded with glee. *Finally I look like someone,* she thought. *What an amazing feeling!*

Carmine encouraged her not to hold anything against Angelina. Stephanie had an amazing childhood, raised by two loving parents who didn't want to lose her.

"When I was a boy, I was tough," he said. "I'm glad you weren't raised like me."

Stephanie's heart ached for the little boy—her brother—who didn't deserve a childhood like that.

Before they hung up, Carmine said almost reverently, "You've saved me."

Stephanie paused. "What do you mean?"

"I was lost," he said. "I've been lost for years. But now? Knowing you're real? That you're out there? That you're willing to talk? I feel like I can breathe again."

"So do I." Stephanie wiped away a tear with a napkin from the table. "What do we do now?" she asked.

Carmine smiled so brightly it came through the phone. "We meet. In person. Soon."

"Yes," she said. "Soon."

They both hesitated, knowing the call was all but over, neither of them wanting to hang up. And the silence that followed felt full—for the first time in both their lives.

"Goodnight, Sis," he said.

"Goodnight, Carmine."

CHAPTER 11:
SIBLING LOVE
(2007)

Stephanie and Carmine planned their first meeting for early September, right after Labor Day. The weeks between their first phone call and the upcoming meeting felt like a lifetime, and for both of them, the anticipation built like a slow, rolling wave. Their excitement was electric, but so was their nervousness.

They had spent hours talking on the phone, texting constantly, emailing photos back and forth, and sharing pieces of their pasts. But seeing each other in person—for the first time—was different.

Stephanie prepared for her brother's visit as if she were welcoming royalty. She cleaned the house twice. She bought fresh flowers, cooked way too much food, and rearranged picture frames. The house smelled of her homemade chocolate chip cookies and buzzed with nervous energy.

Matthew was supportive but cautious. "I'm glad your brother is coming," he said one evening, "but just go slow. There's still a lot you don't know yet. I want you to be safe, and I—I don't want you to be disappointed if Carmine isn't everything you expect him to be." Stephanie only nodded when her husband told her that.

In general, Angelina remained calm, watching from the periphery. The children, especially Gabriella, were excited but confused. "He's your brother?" she asked. "How come I never met him before?"

"Because life is funny sometimes, sweetheart," Stephanie replied. "But now he's coming to meet you." One day she would explain everything to Gabriella and Jonathan, but not now. It was a conversation for when they were older.

On the day Carmine was to arrive, Stephanie stood outside on the porch in jeans and a cream-colored blouse, watching the street, her heart fluttering. She waited nervously, trying not to fidget. Then a black SUV—the one she'd reserved for Carmine at the airport—rolled to a stop in front of her house.

Stephanie held her breath.

Carmine stepped out slowly, squinting at the afternoon sun. He was taller than she expected and more muscular. He had warm, brown eyes that mirrored her own. They hesitated before speaking, holding back just long enough to let the gravity of the moment land.

Then they walked toward one another—quickly, almost skipping—and hugged. They looked intently at each other and smiled. Stephanie thought, *He has my same smile.*

"You look just like her," Carmine said, his voice thick. "Just like our mom."

Stephanie's heart clenched. "And you look like someone I should've known my whole life."

Carmine pulled her in tighter, and Stephanie melted into his embrace. They didn't need words, not just yet.

Inside, Matthew welcomed Carmine warmly with a handshake and a hug. They hit it off right away—two guys from Brooklyn slapping each other's backs, a certain familiarity already between them. The kids were cautious for a moment. They peeked around the corner at first and then broke into smiles, ran to Carmine, and hugged his legs. Gabriella handed him a drawing she'd made of a stick-figure family with her new uncle included. In bright purple crayon, she'd written, "Welcome Uncle Carmine!"

Carmine took the picture from her gently, holding it like it was made of glass. "Thank you." He felt tears welling up, but he managed to hold back for the kids' sake.

Angelina walked up to him and said, "Nice to meet you, Carmine."

Carmine kissed her quickly on each cheek. "So nice to meet you. I've heard so much about you. Thank you for taking care of her and raising her so well." Angelina's eyes glittered at the compliment.

Dinner was full of cheerful, lively conversation. Afterward, Stephanie and Carmine sat together at the dining room table for hours. Stephanie showed him family photo albums, pointing to the canopy bed her dad had made from scratch, her grammar school class photos, her prom pictures, and her wedding-day photos.

Carmine grinned at the little girl in one of the photos. "You looked so happy," he said.

"I was," she admitted, "but I always knew something wasn't right."

Carmine told stories about Cecilia, how funny she was, how she would dance around their kitchen barefoot, how she would belt out Motown songs in her scratchy voice. He told Stephanie about Papa and Nonna—how they'd done their best to provide for him. He talked of Aunt Linda and how she'd taken him in and changed his life.

"Mom could make you laugh and cry in the same breath," Carmine said, proudly showing her a picture in the small photo book he'd brought. Stephanie soaked in the image as if it were water for a parched soul. "She was wild but damaged—beautiful and unpredictable," he continued, his voice drifting off.

They marveled at how much they looked alike in old pictures—like twins separated by time. They stayed up late, talking long after Matthew and the kids had gone to bed. "You were just twenty blocks away," Stephanie said. "I keep thinking that we must have passed each other in stores or sat at the same red lights. We must have walked side by side in the halls of our high school—and probably in so many other places too. Snuck into the same nightclubs, went to the same movie theaters."

"It's crazy," said Carmine. "How could we not have known? We know so many of the same people."

"We got robbed of so much," said Stephanie sadly.

"Ha!" said Carmine. "You wouldn't have liked me if you'd known me back then. I was such a punk. You were a good girl by comparison." He scratched his arm nervously. "Different circles."

The next day, Stephanie, with the kids in tow, showed Carmine around her area of the Jersey Shore. They all strolled along the boardwalk and inhaled the salty air. They ate too much pizza, funnel cake, and ice cream. Carmine had always loved pizza. "Pizza is like a hug. Even when it's sloppy, it's good," he explained. Carmine insisted on winning each of the kids stuffed animals that were bigger than they were. Gabriella and Jonathan howled with delight. Stephanie felt as if she were reclaiming her brother inch by inch.

The next day was the annual Festival of the Sea on Main Street in town with delicious seafood, music, and vendors galore. The residents of Point Pleasant cherished the celebration, and Stephanie had been looking forward to her first time attending as a local and not a touristy "Benny." She was overjoyed to introduce Carmine to her new neighborhood friends, and they were stunned at the resemblance between the two of them. Carmine glowed in a way that made time slow down around him.

Stephanie was happier than she'd ever been, but the weekend visit passed too quickly. When Carmine left, she stood at the door watching his car disappear, tears streaming down her face. She cried for the life they'd never shared and for the new one now blooming.

∞ ∞ ∞

The next trip was Stephanie's in mid-October. She kissed her husband and children goodbye and boarded a flight to Florida by herself. It was strange traveling solo and even stranger knowing that her destination was the home of a brother she'd only just met. She'd packed lightly and brought a framed photo of her and Carmine from that first weekend. She took deep breaths during the landing.

Carmine met her at the airport with open arms and her favorite iced coffee drink. "I figured you'd need this," he said, grinning. He carried her bag and insisted on stopping for Cuban sandwiches on the way home, proudly showing her bits of his world. He took her to every street corner, mural, and neighborhood that meant something to him.

He pointed out the old barbershop he'd once worked in, told her stories about late-night joyrides on his motorcycle, and regaled her with tales of beach bonfires and parties. Stephanie laughed, soaking it all in. Carmine seemed lighter—brighter than when they'd first met.

When they arrived at Carmine's home, Diane greeted Stephanie at the door with a polite smile and cool eyes. "So you're the famous sister," Diane said, offering her hand for a handshake. Diane was beautiful, no doubt, with honey-blonde hair and sharp cheekbones, but her smile was empty, too nice.

Stephanie offered a broad grin and a gentle handshake. "It's really nice to meet you, Diane." She tried to stay positive. She complimented the house, commented on the warm Florida breeze, and helped set the table. She even offered to cook.

For dinner that night, Diane made lasagna and opened a bottle of wine. The meal started with light conversation—funny stories about teen years, family memories, their tastes in music—but things soured quickly. Diane kept interrupting her husband. She corrected Carmine mid-sentence again and again. She rolled her eyes at his jokes.

Stephanie tried to stay focused on her brother. She was here to see him—not Diane—and she tried to lighten things up by talking about a concert she and Carmine had unknowingly both attended as teens.

Diane wasn't having it, her annoyance obviously growing. "We get it," she finally snapped, setting down her fork loudly. "You two found each other. Can we talk about something else?"

The silence at the table was deafening. "Di, don't do this," Carmine pleaded after a long moment.

"I'm just saying," she replied coldly.

Stephanie forced a smile. "Of course," she said calmly. "I didn't mean to dominate the conversation."

After dinner, Carmine and Diane argued behind closed doors. Stephanie sat on the patio listening to the muffled shouting, her last glass of wine untouched. A door slammed. Something fell to the floor. Then silence.

Stephanie wrapped her arms around herself and stared at the stars, feeling very out of place. She missed Matthew and the kids. In that moment, Stephanie wished she was back home with them where there was little drama—her happy home full of love and calmness.

Carmine came outside twenty minutes later, his face flushed, his hands shaking. "I'm sorry," he said. "This isn't how I wanted this to go."

Stephanie reached for his hand. "You don't need to apologize," she replied. "It's okay. I see what's happening. I'm just going to go to a hotel."

"Oh, please don't," Carmine begged. "It's just that—that she's not handling this well. She's angry. She thinks I've changed since I found you, that I don't need her." He ran his hand through his hair. "Ironic since she's the one who hired someone to finally find you."

"She's not wrong," Stephanie said, surprising herself. "You have changed. You've found something that fills the emptiness you had inside. And she's terrified of being pushed out."

Carmine met her eyes. He nodded slowly. "I didn't want to admit it, but yeah. Diane resents you. She blames you for how I've been."

Stephanie watched him, her heart aching. "Do you still love her?"

He didn't answer.

She sighed. "I can't fix your marriage, Carmine. I wish I could. I can only be here for you. I can be your sister and the friend you need. But for tonight, I think it's better for everybody if I go to a hotel."

When Stephanie left that night, Diane didn't say goodbye. Carmine dropped Stephanie off at a hotel nearby, promising to see her for breakfast the next day. He practically wept when he left her at the front desk with her suitcase.

The next morning he picked her up on his motorcycle, and they walked the beach together, barefoot and quiet. The wind whipped at their sleeves. They just walked, the sound of the waves soothing them, the clouds overhead calming them.

When they reached the pier, Carmine leaned on the railing and looked out at the waves. "This is what peace feels like," he said, "just being around you. This feels like home."

Stephanie smiled but stayed silent. She stood beside him, letting the moment settle between them. After a while, she said, "I was hoping to meet Nathan before I fly back. I'm his aunt, after all. Is he with Sarah this weekend?"

Carmine's jaw tightened slightly. "Yeah. She said they had some family thing. She's . . . difficult."

Stephanie glanced at him, sensing the weight behind the word *difficult*. "I'm sorry," she said. "That must be hard."

He nodded. "It is. They're on the west coast of Florida now, and I miss my son more than I can say out loud."

Stephanie reached for his hand and gave it a slight squeeze. Her life was full of ease and connection, and his was tangled in custody schedules and strained conversations.

Stephanie flew home the next day as planned. Another weekend had slipped away too quickly, the tide pulling time forward whether they were ready for it or not.

∞ ∞ ∞

Stephanie met Carmine at Newark Airport with a scarf and gloves. "I bet you forgot how cold it gets up here, didn't you?"

They both laughed. "That's what sisters are for," Carmine said, taking the gifts. "Thanks."

"I'm so glad you could come for Thanksgiving!" she said, meaning it.

"Yeah, it all worked out nicely," Carmine said. "Sarah wants Nathan with her for the long weekend, and Diane and her kids are going to her parents' house for the holiday."

"Perfect!" Stephanie squealed, "And my kids are so excited to see you again."

Stephanie sized up her brother as he wrapped his scarf around his neck. He looked better than when she'd left him—calmer somehow.

When they arrived at the house, Gabriella ran into Carmine's arms. Jonathan handed him a tiny felt turkey he had made by hand. "For you, Uncle Carmine."

That night, Carmine and Stephanie stayed up late cooking traditional Thanksgiving side dishes and laughing over bad TV. He looked around the large but cozy kitchen and said, "I could get used to this."

Everyone from Brooklyn would be there tomorrow—cousins, aunts, uncles, and old friends. Stephanie wanted Carmine to meet everyone, and it was her family's first Thanksgiving in their new home. She'd gone all out—fall garland on the mantle, pumpkin pies cooling on the windowsill, and as many folding chairs as she could manage to find.

Stephanie was up early Thanksgiving morning, getting out of bed even before Carmine. She started roasting the turkey at 8:00 a.m. and placed little name cards on the table for her guests. Carmine's card said "Uncle Carmine" in Gabriella's handwriting, and it was placed at the head of the table.

Carmine asked Matthew to take him shopping while Stephanie and Angelina were busy with the turkey and last-minute details. He bought Stephanie's favorite flowers—

lilies in all colors—for the table, along with a nice bottle of Chianti.

He even dressed up, wearing a button-down shirt and dress shoes. "I packed for the occasion. I wanted to do it right," he said.

"You already are." Stephanie beamed.

As the guests began to arrive, Stephanie's family welcomed Carmine with open arms. Her cousin Maria immediately sat down next to him. "So this is the brother," she said, giving him a hug. "You two look so much alike." She pulled out of the embrace. "Tell me—what's it like having her for a sister?" Everyone laughed.

Carmine told stories like the one about Cecilia teaching the neighbor's parrot to sing Sinatra just to annoy the landlord. He had the room in stitches by the time he was done.

Aunt Arlene wept openly at the sight of them together. "I'm so glad you two finally found each other," she said through her tears. She knew how hard it was for all of them, the whole family, to have kept this secret for four decades. It was how Angelina and Jack needed things to be, but the weight of it had been a deep burden for everyone else.

It was a chaotic and joyful day—laughter overlapping conversations, second helpings, and clinking glasses—a house so full of love. Even Angelina was joyful for the first time since Stephanie had learned about the adoption. At one point, Carmine looked around the room, holding his glass in his hand. Stephanie noticed happy tears glistening in his eyes. In a hushed tone, he said to her, "This is what it's supposed to feel like."

After dessert, Carmine and Matthew stood by the sink doing dishes. Matthew handed him a dish towel and nodded toward his wife who was curled up on the couch laughing with her cousins.

"She's been floating on air since you came into her life," Matthew said.

Carmine looked over to him. "I feel the same way. Being here today—knowing her—means a lot, man. Thanks for everything."

Later that night, after everyone had gone, Carmine and Stephanie, wrapped in sweatshirts and nursing leftover wine, sat together on the back patio. The firepit had just started to dwindle, and the silence between them was precious.

"I don't want to go back," he said finally.

Stephanie turned to him, her eyes soft.

"I've decided that I'm leaving Diane," he continued. "We're breaking up for good this time. I can't live in that chaos anymore, and her kids are old enough to understand. I want to be here near you and start over—start living the life we were supposed to have."

Stephanie's eyes filled with tears. She placed a hand on his shoulder. "I'd love that."

"I want to be part of your life, really be part of it and be an uncle to your kids," he continued. "I want to come to Sunday dinner, help Matthew fix things around the house, and be the brother I was supposed to be. I want a second chance—maybe even open up my own barbershop." He exhaled deeply like he'd been holding that single breath for years.

Stephanie squeezed his hand. "Then do it. Life's short, and we've lost enough time."

They sat in silence for a while, staring at the dying flames.

"Do you think we've missed too much time?" he asked.

"I think we've just begun," Stephanie answered.

CHAPTER 12:
In the Blink of an Eye (2007)

On his return flight to Florida, Carmine was a changed man. He was full from love, full of hope, and eager to move his life forward.

Diane greeted him at the baggage claim with her arms folded and mouth tight. She didn't say much on the drive home, but the silence between them was laced with resentment. She could feel that something had tilted, and not in her favor. The way Carmine looked at her—like he was searching for someone else behind her eyes—was proof.

At a red light on the way home, Diane glanced sideways. "You're quieter," she said.

Carmine kept his gaze on the windshield. "I'm just tired." The lie hung in the air like humidity—thick and murky.

At home in their bedroom, Diane watched her husband unpack, his movements deliberate like he was trying not to disturb something fragile.

"You didn't bring me anything," she said, half joking.

Carmine looked up, confused. "What?"

"Bring me something from Jersey. A souvenir. A magnet. A crumb of whatever made you so happy up there."

He opened his mouth and then closed it. "I didn't think to."

Any hint of a joke dissipated as Diane's temper surged. "Exactly."

For a few days, the warmth of the Thanksgiving celebration lingered in Carmine's soul. He texted Stephanie every morning with updates—ideas for his barbershop's logo; jokes about how he'd need long johns if he moved back north; mentions of Bensonhurst parks, pizza joints, and bakeries from their childhood that he hoped they would visit together someday. Stephanie invited him to Gabriella's school recital and referred to their future trip together as the "Brooklyn nostalgia tour"—complete with bagels, subway transfers, and heartburn—and reminded him daily that she loved him, that they all loved him.

Carmine promised that he wouldn't let the feeling between them—between him, Stephanie, and her whole family—fade. He would leave Diane. He would move to New Jersey and start again.

A few days later, Carmine stood in the backyard, a mug of coffee cooling in his hand. He stared at the fence line. The neighbor's dog barked. A sprinkler hissed to life. He didn't move. Diane watched him from the kitchen window, arms crossed.

"I thought you were gonna stand there all day," she said when he came back in.

He shrugged. "I was just thinking."

"About what?" Diane asked.

He ignored her question and walked out of the room.

Later, he sent a text to Stephanie: "Started looking at apartments. Found a place near Red Bank. I like the vibe there. Big windows. Feels like a fresh start."

Carmine started keeping a notebook, a cheap spiral-bound thing from a gas station. Inside he scribbled plans—barbershop names, sketches of logos, lists of things he would need to buy. Diane found it one morning on the kitchen counter while he was showering. She flipped through it, her eyes narrowing.

Carmine walked in a few minutes later, a towel around his neck. Diane pointed to the notebook. "Carmine's Cuts? Northside Fades? What's this?" she demanded.

"Ideas," he replied.

"For what?"

"For goals," he said. Diane didn't ask what that meant. She didn't ask if she was part of those goals.

Carmine and Stephanie continued to call each other or talk over text every day. But beneath all the hopeful sibling chatter was a heaviness Carmine couldn't shake. He'd had a glimpse of the life he'd never had, and suddenly the life he'd built for himself didn't fit anymore. Everything in Florida felt stale—the house, the marriage, step-fatherhood, the hallway lined with old photos of smiles that hadn't been real in years.

"You were different when you got back," Diane said the next night, "like your body came home but your heart didn't."

"It's different up north," Carmine answered.

"Different how?" Diane challenged.

"Just different," he mumbled.

Diane walked out of the room in frustration.

Carmine had only been home a week when the storms began. Nothing in his life felt right anymore, but Diane wasn't giving him an inch. He tried to explain and reason with her, but she didn't understand—couldn't understand. All Diane knew was that every day that passed she was losing her husband—her whole life—to some faraway family.

Two nights later, Carmine was sitting on the edge of the bed, his elbows on his knees, when Diane walked in. "I'm not trying to hurt you," he said.

Diane crossed her arms. "You already did."

"I just feel like I need something different, something I should have had all along."

"Different from me?" she said, almost pleading.

He looked up. "Different from this."

She had no words. She just turned off the light, leaving her husband sitting alone in the dark.

Carmine didn't sleep that night. He lay there staring at the ceiling, listening to Diane's breathing from the other side of the bed. Slow. Steady. Indifferent.

At 3:17 a.m., he got up and wandered into the kitchen. The tile floor was cold under his feet. He opened the fridge, not for food but for the light. It spilled out across the floor, casting long shadows that made the room feel cavernous. He poured himself a glass of water and then dumped it down the sink.

In the living room, he sat on the couch and looked through photos in an album that Stephanie had put together for him. Her kids. The Thanksgiving table. A blurry shot of the two of them in front of the aquarium on the boardwalk, both laughing, heads tilted together like they hadn't missed a beat.

He played one of Stephanie's voicemails. "Morning, Carmine. Just thinking about you. Hope today feels a little lighter. Call me if you need anything, okay?"

"I need everything," he said to the empty room.

The next morning, Diane found her husband still on the couch, his eyes open, his face blank.

"You didn't come to bed," she said.

"I did for a little while," he replied. "But I couldn't find the part of me that used to fit."

Diane didn't ask what that meant. She didn't want to know. "Thank God the kids are back at school," she said. "They can't see you like this."

Carmine stood up and grabbed his pillow, but then he paused. "I'm not asking you to be happy for me," he said. "I'm asking you to stop punishing me."

Diane, now at the kitchen island with her fingers curled around a chipped mug she hadn't bothered to fill, replied. "You think I'm punishing you?" she asked. "You think this is punishment?"

Carmine followed her into the kitchen and poured himself a cup of coffee. He watched the steam rise from it as if the wisps held the words he couldn't find.

"I'm trying to understand," she said, sitting down at the island. "I really am. But every time I ask you to explain, you give me riddles. You say it's not about her; it's about you. You say you feel different. You say you're not trying to hurt me, but you never say what you want."

"I want to feel whole," he replied. "I want to stop pretending."

Diane's laugh was bitter and brief. "Pretending? Is that what this was?"

"No," he said, "but it became that somewhere along the way."

She set her mug down hard, making a spoon on the island rattle. "I didn't sign up to share you with someone else," she snapped.

"She's my sister, Diane, not another woman. My sister!"

"She's a stranger. A fantasy. You'd throw away our life for someone you've known five minutes?" she screamed.

"Because I finally feel like I know who I am."

Diane stormed out, unable—or unwilling—to listen anymore.

Stephanie for her part tried to stay supportive from afar. She offered to help Carmine find apartments, jobs, anything. When they talked, Carmine always sounded grateful but worn thin. He told Stephanie he was just tired, but in truth he was lost in an internal tug-of-war. Up north he felt seen. Down south he felt haunted.

Two weeks after Carmine got home, he started drinking—not in the celebratory way he had during his first trip to New Jersey but in a desperate way. Stephanie could hear it in his voice. His texts came less often, and when they did, they were short, sometimes cryptic. Stephanie tried not to worry. She reminded herself that change takes time. She told herself that it had only been a few weeks—a matter of days. She tried not to listen to the little voice inside telling her something was wrong.

Diane stopped asking Carmine where he had gone when he went out and stopped looking when he drank alone in the house. She just noted the smell, the thickness of his speech, and the way he forgot what day it was.

The tension between them grew. It was a Monday night when Carmine glared at Diane from across the kitchen island, the overhead light exaggerating the exhaustion in his face.

"What's wrong now?" she asked.

"I'm just thinking," he said.

"About leaving?" she asked.

He sighed but didn't answer. Diane knew his silence was answer enough.

The fighting continued hard and fast. Every night ended in shouting. She accused him of emotional abandonment. He accused her of resentment. One night Diane smashed a picture frame. The next night, Carmine packed a duffel bag, only to unpack it two hours later.

Stephanie stayed neutral. She encouraged her brother to make decisions for his peace, not out of anger. She told him to take care of himself, to come back up north whenever he was ready. She put as little pressure on him as possible, even though she was eager for him to move.

She started saving her brother's voicemails, just in case. She replayed his messages. "Yo, it's me. Just checking in. Hope today's better than yesterday. I'm really trying." "Steph, Gabriella's recital video made me cry. Don't tell her that. Tell her the snowman with the mustache is going on my fridge." "Love you. Don't forget." Stephanie never told Carmine she was saving his voicemails, but she couldn't delete them either, not even the ones where he sounded tired—especially not those.

Carmine started sleeping in the guest room. For a solid week, he spent more nights out than in. Friends appeared—the type of friends who partied. Cocaine, whiskey, drag racing, and late-night confessions to bartenders who weren't listening consumed his nights. He could see himself slipping, see his mother's worst coming out in him, but he couldn't control it. He couldn't stop.

It was a Saturday night when Carmine came home with a busted lip. “What happened?” Diane asked.

“Bar fight,” he muttered.

“Over what?”

“Nothing. Everything.”

She handed him an ice pack. He didn’t thank her. They sat in the kitchen in silence, the ice pack dripping slowly onto the floor, each drop louder than the words they couldn’t say.

Carmine started driving aimlessly, stopping often at gas stations for coffee and cigarettes in brands he didn’t smoke. Sometimes he parked at the beach and stared out at the waves, wondering if he’d ever feel whole again. The ocean didn’t offer any solutions. It never did.

On one drunken night, Carmine called Stephanie, slurring his words. “I don’t think I’ll make it to forty,” he said. “Make sure they play ‘Into the Mystic’ by Van Morrison at my funeral.”

“Don’t say that,” she replied sharply. “You’re just upset. You have a lot going on, and you’re trying to make a permanent decision. You’re being too hard on yourself. You’re tired, but you’ll get through this.”

“I’m serious,” he said. “I’ve never seen myself past forty. Not once. Not in a dream. Not in a thought. It’s like my clock runs out there.”

Stephanie sat up in bed, her heart pounding. “Carmine, don’t talk like that, please. Remember we discussed having a big fortieth birthday party for you here? My forty-first and your fortieth, together. All the family. Great food, a DJ, dancing, and everything. It was your idea.” She paused to wipe a tear from her cheek. “You promised,” she pleaded, barely getting the words out.

Carmine mumbled something unintelligible and hung up.

She called back. No answer. With the phone still in her hand, she stared at the ceiling for a long while.

A little while later, Matthew stirred beside her. "Everything okay?"

She hesitated. "Carmine's not okay."

"You want me to call him?" he asked.

She shook her head. "He won't listen. Not to anyone. Not now at least."

Stephanie got up and went to the living room where she sat down, wrapped herself in a blanket, and began staring off into space. She stayed on the sofa the whole night, not sleeping.

The next morning, Carmine texted a simple message: "Sorry. Rough night. Love you. Don't forget."

Stephanie breathed a small sigh of relief. Maybe Carmine would be open to talking later. Maybe it had just been a bad mood. Maybe it had just been his insecurities talking.

With Christmas less than a week away, Carmine lost his job at the warehouse. He'd shown up late too many times and smelled like liquor almost every day for a week. The owner, a friend since he had first moved to Florida, told him it wasn't personal, but it was final.

When Carmine called Stephanie to tell her the bad news, she begged him to come north early, to spend Christmas with her and her family, but he said no. "It's not time yet," he answered, even though he longed for another visit. "I still gotta handle things down here. I have Nathan to think about too."

Almost one month to the day after Thanksgiving, on Friday December 21, Stephanie mailed Carmine's Christmas present—long johns, a photo of the kids, and a handwritten card that said, "Whenever you're ready, your family is here." She paid extra for shipping to ensure the package would arrive by Christmas Eve.

While she was busy at the post office, Carmine and Diane were fighting. They'd been at it all day—the same argument, just in a different form.

When it was time for bed, Carmine locked himself in the bathroom just to get away from Diane. He splashed cold water on his face and then gripped the sink like it might anchor him.

Diane banged on the door. "You think you're the only one who's suffering?"

He stared at his reflection. Bloodshot eyes. Jaw clenched. "I don't know who I am anymore."

Diane kept yelling, but he didn't hear her, not really. As soon as Carmine opened the bathroom door, she confronted him. She had found an apartment listing in his email.

"You're really gonna leave me? After all I've done for you?" she screamed. "I'm the one who found her for you. And this is how you repay me?"

"I've already left," he muttered, pushing past her and making his way down the hall.

"Don't walk away from me, Carmine."

He turned, his face red with rage. "I have nothing left here, Diane. You hate me. Your kids hate me. I hate this life. I'm done."

The door slammed behind him. Diane followed her husband outside but paused in the doorframe.

The Florida night was sticky and dark. The neighbors heard shouting—then something shattering.

Carmine scrambled into his car and clenched the steering wheel, his knuckles turning white. He revved the engine so hard that it sounded as angry as he was.

Diane, barefoot and furious, ran to the driveway and yanked the passenger door open. "You wanna run? Fine! But you're not leaving me behind." She clambered in, still shouting. Carmine, exhausted from his lack of sleep and hours of fighting, let her rant.

The tires screeched as Carmine surged out of the driveway.

They sped through the serene streets of Fort Lauderdale, their silence now more dangerous than words. Diane fumbled with her seat belt, but it didn't click in.

"Slow down!" she yelled as they hit 70 miles per hour.

Carmine didn't listen. Instead, he pulled onto the highway and increased his speed.

"Where are we going?!" Diane screamed. "You're speeding to get nowhere!"

They stayed on the highway for at least an hour, their toxic relationship filling the silence. Carmine sped on, watching the oncoming headlights whizz by as he pushed the engine even more. With the gas pedal to the floor, the car started to shake.

"Slow down, Carmine! You're going to be the death of us both!"

Carmine barely heard his wife. He was in a trance, his anger and frustration consuming him. The contrast between what was and what could have been had become too sharp, like a knife stuck in his chest.

With little real idea of where he was going, Carmine pulled off the highway into Port St. Lucie, an area he didn't know well, but he knew it would bring him to the coast.

Off the highway, Carmine tore through the dark streets, eventually hitting 90 miles per hour. The clock ticked toward 2:00 a.m.

Diane screamed at Carmine again to slow down, breaking the silence for the first time since they'd exited the highway. It startled him.

A squeal of the brakes. A distant scream. A sickening metallic crash. The car crumpled against the trunk of a palm tree like a crushed soda can.

Diane ejected through the passenger side windshield and flew out of the car, landing several yards away in a mangled sprawl of limbs and blood. A few people who had heard the crash began gathering on the street. With what little strength she had, Diane managed to squeak out, "Call 911."

Carmine, bloody and limp, didn't move—not even when a good Samaritan tried to wake him; not when Diane called to him with her weak, hoarse voice; not when the fire department arrived; and not when the EMTs placed him on the gurney.

CHAPTER 13:
The Cleaving (2007)

Stephanie sat down in the kitchen, cradling her cup of coffee. The house was wrapped in the sleepy stillness of a Saturday morning. The Christmas shopping was all done, and the weekend sprawled before her lazy and free with the possibility of taking the kids sledding tomorrow if it snowed overnight.

The phone rang, shattering the morning's quiet. Stephanie jumped.

She answered on the second ring. "Hello?"

"Is this Stephanie DeRosa?" The voice was male, steady but too calm.

"Yes. Who is this?"

"This is Officer Thompson with the Florida Highway Patrol." Stephanie froze as the officer continued. "I'm very sorry to inform you that your brother, Carmine Esposito, was involved in a motor vehicle accident last night." He paused as if steeling himself. "I regret to tell you he did not survive."

Time stopped. The stillness in the room transformed from peaceful to terrifying.

"I'm sorry—what? What do you mean 'did not survive'?" Stephanie's desperation had crept into her tone. "There's some mistake. My brother is in Fort Lauderdale. He's fine. He just called me two days ago."

"I'm sorry," Officer Thompson said again. "It was a single-vehicle crash at high speed. He was pronounced dead at the scene."

Stephanie dropped her mug. It shattered as it hit the floor.

"No!" she gasped. "No, no, no!"

"I understand this is difficult." Officer Thompson hesitated for a moment and then softened his tone and continued. "It was quick. The EMTs said that with his injuries, he never stood a chance."

Pain punched her in the chest as reality set in. "God, no. God, please," she gasped as if her lungs were too small. "How can this be happening?"

"There was another passenger in the vehicle: Diane Esposito. She was ejected from the car and has been transported to St. Lucie Medical Center. She's in intensive care."

Stephanie didn't hear the rest. The phone slipped out of her hand and hit the hardwood floor with a hollow clatter.

She followed, sinking to the floor. Her scream woke the entire house.

Frantic, Matthew ran into the room. Stephanie, curled in on herself and gulping for oxygen like the air had turned to smoke, couldn't speak. She couldn't say the words out loud.

"What is it?" Matthew asked. "Steph?" He crouched beside her, helpless. "Stephanie, talk to me. Please!"

She shook her head violently, her fists pressed to her temples. "No. No. No! Not him. Not now!"

Seeing the phone on the floor, Matthew picked it up and spoke to the officer briefly. His spine stiffened as he was told the news. "Thank you for informing us, officer," he said in an even but forced voice before he hung up. Tears stung Matthew's eyes.

Startled by the noise, the dog in the backyard next door started barking. Stephanie barely heard it. A neighbor knocked on the door, concerned, but neither Stephanie nor Matthew could answer it.

Screaming into her hands, Stephanie folded even farther into herself. Matthew went to hold her, but she writhed away, not ready to be touched.

The hours that followed were a whirlwind. Phone calls. Questions. Logistics. Shock.

Angelina clutched her rosary all day, whispering to herself, whispering to God. "No," she breathed. "Not him. Not like this."

Maria rushed over with coffee and a crumb cake, sat on the couch, and held her cousin's hand without saying a word. Stephanie sobbed into her knees. "He just got here, Maria." she cried. "We just found each other. He was only thirty-nine!" She cried for hours. Maria sat next to her the whole time.

At one point, Stephanie wandered into the laundry room and saw Carmine's gray Harley Davidson sweatshirt folded on the shelf that hung over the washing machine. He'd left it behind on his visit, and Stephanie had put it there to give to him when he came back. She picked it up slowly and pressed it to her face, searching for his scent.

Maria watched from the doorway, tears streaming silently. “You don’t have to be strong,” she said.

“I’m not,” Stephanie murmured. “I’m broken.”

The kids didn’t understand. Gabriella asked if Uncle Carmine was still coming for Christmas. Stephanie’s heart broke all over again.

Later that night, Stephanie sat on the den floor where Carmine had stayed, feeling as though the room was still full of his energy. She clutched the photo they’d taken on the boardwalk that first weekend. Her smile looked different to her now.

The days that followed were drenched in fog. Stephanie called Aunt Arlene. She phoned Aunt Linda’s husband, Anthony, so he could tell the twins. She tried calling Carmine’s friends in Florida, starting with his old boss in the warehouse who gave her a few other numbers. But half the time, she couldn’t finish her sentences when she talked to them. She notified Lisa, the genealogist who’d brought them together, who wept openly with her over the phone.

Nights were the worst. Not sleeping, Stephanie opened her phone and scrolled through their last texts. “You’d love this diner. Real Jersey vibes.” “Thinking about getting a tattoo. Nothing huge. Maybe a barber’s razor. Or maybe we should get matching tattoos when I come up there. How about our initials intertwined?” “Love you. Don’t forget.”

Two nights after the news came, Stephanie stared at her phone until it blurred. Then she typed a message she knew Carmine would never read: “I miss you. Please come back.”

Officer Thompson called back the following morning. Carmine's body was being held in a morgue in St. Lucie County. Diane had several broken bones along with severe facial fractures. She'd been thrown from the car and found nearly thirty feet away in the grass.

Even though she wanted to, Stephanie didn't reach out to Diane. She knew Diane wouldn't welcome her call.

The funeral was set for December 27 in Florida.

Stephanie went through the motions on Christmas for her children's sake and then flew down to Florida the next day with Matthew by her side. Angelina volunteered to stay home with the kids. With her advancing years, traveling in the middle of winter felt like too much.

On the plane, Stephanie clutched the armrest during takeoff, her eyes closed. Matthew reached over. "You alright?"

She nodded, but her voice cracked as she answered. "I feel like I'm flying toward the end of something."

∞ ∞ ∞

The memorial was held in a simple chapel near the ocean in Lauderdale-by-the-Sea. White pews. Pale blue carpet. An altar lined with candles. "Into the Mystic" played in the background.

Only a handful of mourners came: Uncle Anthony and the twins, two or three other cousins, some old friends, two barbers from the shop where Carmine used to work, a few co-workers from the warehouse. Sarah didn't come, and neither did Nathan. Stephanie wondered why, although she didn't ask.

Diane arrived late in a wheelchair, escorted by a nurse and flanked on either side by her children, Melissa and Sam.

A shocked murmur spread throughout the room when she appeared. Her left eye was bruised, and her arm was in a cast. She didn't speak to Stephanie.

Stephanie stood near the front of the chapel, staring at the closed casket. She placed a single red rose on top. She lingered there, running her fingertips along the polished wood. "I hope you know how much you were loved," she whispered. "I hope you felt it, even if only for a second."

Stephanie turned from the casket and found herself face-to-face with a man who smelled faintly of aftershave. His eyes were bloodshot, his hands rough, his arms muscled and solid under his suit.

"Are you Stephanie?" he asked gently.

She nodded, wiping her cheek.

"I'm Tommy. Carmine worked with me at the warehouse. I just wanted to say that he talked about you all the time, like you were some kind of miracle."

Stephanie's breath caught. "He did?"

"Every damn day," Tommy said, his voice cracking. "He showed me pictures and told me about your kids. He was so proud to be an uncle. He said he finally felt like he belonged somewhere."

Another man, this one tall and wiry with salt-and-pepper stubble and a voice like gravel, stepped forward. "I'm Dean. We used to grab beers after work. He was stubborn as a bull but loyal. If he loved you, you knew it."

Stephanie smiled faintly. "He was all of that."

Tommy looked down at the carpet and then back up. "He was trying, you know, to be better, to build something. He told us about his plans for a shop. He said he wanted to open a place with his name on the window."

Stephanie's eyes welled again. "Yes, I think he was going to call it Carmine's Cuts."

Dean reached into his jacket and pulled out a small, folded piece of paper. "He gave me this the day before the crash. It's a list of names to put on the chairs in the new shop. He wanted each station to be named after someone he loved."

Stephanie took the paper with shaking hands. She was there, scribbled in Carmine's handwriting. "Chair One: Sis."

She pressed the paper to her chest, thanking him profusely.

The chapel director appeared and asked everyone to take their seats. The priest spoke briefly, ending his remarks with a prayer. A few people shared stories.

When it was her turn, Stephanie stepped up to the podium. She didn't have a speech prepared. All she had was a heart full of memories and a voice shaking with grief.

"I only had a few months with Carmine in my life," she said, her voice trembling. "But in those months, he became my family—a brother, a friend, and a piece of my soul that had been missing my whole life." She swallowed a lump in her throat. "He was funny. And wounded. And stubborn. And generous. He carried more pain than anyone I've ever known, but he also carried hope." She paused. "I was separated from our parents at birth. When Carmine learned about me, he searched for me. He found me and gave me a gift I can never repay: He made me whole." She looked out at the crowd. With eyes full of hate, Diane glared at her but didn't interrupt. Stephanie took a deep breath, trying to ignore her. "I just wish—I wish I'd had more time."

After the service, Stephanie asked Matthew to drive her to the site of the crash. The bark on the tree was splintered and stained. Someone had taped flowers to its base. A small wooden cross with Carmine's name etched in black marker was pressed into the soil.

Stephanie kneeled in the grass and traced the letters of her brother's name. Matthew kept his hand lovingly on her shoulder.

Stephanie pulled a folded photo from her purse—Carmine holding Gabriella on his shoulders, both of them laughing. She tucked it behind the cross, anchoring it with a stone.

"I'll keep your memory alive. I'll keep telling our story," she said, "even the messy parts. Especially those." She choked back a sob. "This shouldn't have been the end. We were just beginning."

Stephanie kneeled at the roadside memorial, weeping until Matthew pulled her away slowly, gently. "Steph, it's time to go," he said as softly as he could.

Later at the hotel, Stephanie sat on the edge of the bed, still in her black dress, staring at the untouched room-service tray. Matthew came out of the bathroom, drying his hands. "Honey, do you want to eat something?"

She shook her head. "I feel like if I eat, it means the day's over. And I don't want it to be. I don't want to leave him behind."

Matthew sat down beside her.

"At the service, I kept thinking he'd walk in," she said, "that he'd make some joke about the priest's accent or the candles. That he'd say, 'Stop crying, will ya, Sis?'"

"My heart aches for you," Matthew said, his voice full of empathy.

"I kept hoping he'd see how much he mattered," she said, "mattered to us, to me."

Well after the sun had set, Stephanie left the hotel to walk along the beach alone—the same beach where she'd walked with Carmine that morning in October. She stood at the edge of the pier, the ocean shimmering in the moonlight. "You're free now, Carmine."

She closed her eyes and let the wind whip her hair across her face.

She said out into the ocean, "I'll pray for you. I'll carry you in my heart always, even when it hurts."

∞ ∞ ∞

The house was quiet when Stephanie awoke. The Christmas tree still stood in the living room, and the grief came in waves.

She walked into the kitchen and opened the pantry. Everything was still labeled—pasta, rice, snacks—exactly the way Carmine used to tease her about.

She pulled out the jar of coffee and paused, realizing that the mug Carmine had used on his visits, the one with the faded Knicks logo—the one he loved—was still in the cabinet. She took it down and held it for a long time before pouring her coffee into it. She missed the way he said Sis like it meant "safety." She missed the way he always signed his texts: "Love you. Don't forget."

She kept hearing his voice—his laughing in the kitchen, his teasing her over the little things. She heard his footsteps on the porch. His deep chuckle on the phone echoed in her mind.

She carried his sweatshirt around the house, not ready to let him go. Everywhere she looked he was there, and yet he was nowhere at all.

Matthew held Stephanie every night as she cried. "He knew," she muttered through her tears each night. "He told me he wouldn't make it to forty."

She went through periods of deep sadness, anger, and numbness. She replayed every phone call, every text, every moment.

A few nights after they returned home, Stephanie, unable to sleep, opened her phone and went to her saved voicemails. Carmine's voice came through the speaker, casual and warm. "Yo, Sis. Just checking in. You'd better be feeding those kids real food and not just bagels. Call me back. Love ya."

She played the message three times. Then again. Then once more, just to hear the way he said Sis.

She blamed herself for not calling more, for not doing enough to support him. She blamed Diane. She blamed fate. She blamed God. But mostly she ached from missing him.

She framed the sketch of Carmine's dream barbershop that he made at Thanksgiving and hung it in the hallway. Every time she passed it, she touched the corner like a ritual.

"I should have made him come and visit again," she said to her cousin Maria through her tears one night. "If he had been here with me, he wouldn't have been in the car with Diane."

"He was so happy he found you, Stephanie. You gave him love," Maria comforted. "You gave him a real family. You gave him some peace before the end."

"Stephanie nodded, finding some comfort in the word *peace.*

Angelina sobbed that night, saying, "I knew something terrible would happen. That boy never got a fair shot." She reached for her daughter's hand, but Stephanie pulled away.

"You don't get to comfort me now, Mom. Everything's changed."

And then, one day toward the end of the year, the package Stephanie had mailed before the crash came back. It was marked as return to sender. The words felt cruel, calculated.

She opened it, hands trembling. Inside was the card she had written. "Whenever you're ready, your family is here."

She sat down on the floor and sobbed. Gabriella found her there an hour later, still clutching the card. "Mommy?"

Stephanie looked up, her eyes swollen. She wiped her cheeks and tried to smile.

Gabriella crawled into her lap and said in her small voice, "I miss him too."

CHAPTER 14:

What Remained (2008)

The days passed achingly slowly. Stephanie was numb, as if she were drifting through life. Everywhere she looked she saw Carmine's ghost.

The den still smelled faintly of him. His extra toothbrush was still in the upstairs bathroom. She felt like she couldn't escape him, but at the same time she didn't want to escape. It felt impossible that someone so full of life could be gone, just like that.

One crash. One moment. One phone call.

She found herself obsessed with listening to Carmine's last voicemail on repeat—his voice sad and thick like he'd been drinking. "I just wanted you to know I love you, Sis. No matter what." Every day, three—maybe four—times a day, she listened to it and then pressed the phone to her chest, rocking it like a mother cradling a child.

She felt like she was becoming him, like all the trauma that had filled Carmine's life was being passed onto her. She didn't know how to carry it—didn't know how to express it, not even to Matthew.

As the days passed, her shock started hardening into anger.

Angry at herself—for not making Carmine move north.

Angry at Diane—for every fight, for every delay, for surviving when he hadn't.

Angry at Angelina—for the years of lies.

Angry at God—for bringing them together only to rip Carmine away.

Her rage, as sharp and dangerous as a new razor blade, came out in shards. It cut through her silences as she lashed out at anyone who tried to help.

She yelled at Maria for picking up the wrong brand of coffee. She snapped at Gabriella when she left her shoes in the hallway. Whenever Jonathan tried to hug her, she stiffened, not able to let her own son in. She tore into Matthew for asking if she wanted to go to church.

"I don't want a sermon," she barked. "I don't want candles or Communion or a priest telling me this is part of God's plan."

Matthew didn't push. He just stood there looking at her with a kind of helpless sorrow she couldn't bear.

Angelina, though, got the worst of it. Stephanie criticized her relentlessly for little things, which started bickering sessions. But the most explosive of their fights came the day they were in the living room sorting through Carmine's photos, trying at first to put together an album for the kids. Stephanie wanted to do it. She said it might help—that maybe organizing memories would make the loss feel less disordered.

But then she found a picture of Carmine as a child—missing a tooth, grinning at the camera, wearing a worn baseball cap. Suddenly Stephanie's fury shot through her, and she couldn't contain herself.

"You let this happen!" she hissed.

Angelina looked up, startled. "What are you talking about?"

"You kept him from me. That's what I'm talking about." Her voice cracked. "I should've had my brother for thirty-nine years, but I didn't—because of you!"

"I promised your father—"

"—He's not my father!" Stephanie shouted. "He's the man who raised me in a lie!"

Angelina's face turned pale as if she'd been slapped. "Don't say that," she begged. "Your father loved you more than anything."

"You *could've* told me. You *should've* told me. I asked you for *years*." Stephanie's voice cracked again. "You looked me in the face, decade after decade, and denied me my family."

Angelina sat back slowly, her hands trembling in her lap. She looked as if she were about to speak, but only a sad sigh of resignation came out.

"I deserved to know," Stephanie continued through gritted teeth. "I could've had him my whole life, but I only got what—four months? Four months of having a brother." She gulped in a breath. "You could've told me at any time—at literally any point in my life—and it would've been better than *this*."

Angelina began crying. "I loved you. I did what I thought was right."

"No. You did what was easiest for you," Stephanie countered. "You kept us apart. And now he's dead." She stood abruptly and turned her back on her mother. "You hid the truth so deep that you forgot there were lives down there. You buried us!"

A silence settled between them for a long moment.

"I accepted Carmine, welcomed him into the family with open arms," Angelina said finally. "I did. I tried."

"I know," Stephanie said, turning around. "But it was too late. He didn't grow up with the love of two parents like I did. His mother was chronically depressed and an addict. He didn't grow up protected. He didn't get what I got. And now he's gone."

Tears slipped down Angelina's cheeks. "I didn't love him the way you loved him. I didn't know how. But I didn't want him to suffer."

"But he did suffer," Stephanie cried. "And I can't stop seeing it."

Angelina stood up. "I'm sorry."

"I know," Stephanie said sarcastically. "But that doesn't change what happened." She stormed upstairs, slamming the bedroom door.

That night, Stephanie cried into her pillow until her body shook with grief. The next morning, she avoided her mother completely.

The weeks dragged. Her marriage began to fray under the weight of her sorrow. Matthew tried to hold them together, but Stephanie's anger seeped into everything.

Matthew took some time off work to care for the family. He cooked dinner. He picked the kids up from school. He kept the house running while Stephanie slunk through it like a shadow.

He gave her space at first, but space turned into silence. Silence turned into absence. Stephanie stopped confiding in him, stopped saying "I love you" at night. She rolled away when he reached for her. She hated what she was becoming, but she didn't know how to stop it.

One night while she was sitting on the back patio wrapped in Carmine's sweatshirt, Matthew joined her with a blanket and two mugs of tea. "I miss you," he said. "I know you're hurting, and I know I can't fix it. But I want to help."

"Do you know what it's like to lose a brother you only just found? What if you had another sibling that everyone kept from you?" she replied.

"No, I can't even imagine it," he said. "But I know what it's like to lose the woman I love a little more every day."

Stephanie stared into the distance. "You want to help? Then bring him back."

Matthew's face fell. "You know I can't."

"Then there's nothing to talk about."

Matthew went inside, the screen door creaking shut behind him. Stephanie cried into Carmine's sweatshirt, feeling even more alone than ever.

∞ ∞ ∞

It was well into spring when the headstone was complete. Stephanie flew down to Florida with Gabriella and Jonathan to visit Carmine's grave. The headstone was simple, as he would have wanted it—black granite etched with his full name: Carmine Leo Esposito, March 11, 1967–December 22, 2007. Beneath it was a single line: "You were loved, you are loved still."

They placed a bouquet of lilies on the grave, and Stephanie read aloud a letter she had written.

Dear Carmine,

You were only here for a short time, but you changed everything.

I wish I'd known you sooner. I wish I could have protected you.

But I'm grateful for what we had. You gave me the truth. You gave me love.

You gave me a brother.

Rest easy now. I will carry you with me, always.

Love,
Your Sis

Stephanie stood there with her children and murmured prayers she didn't know she still believed in. She kneeled in the grass and asked God to send her a sign, anything to help her carry this pain, this absence.

Jonathan left behind a drawing of a man with big muscles and a cape. "That's Uncle Carmine," he said. "He's a superhero now."

Stephanie smiled through her tears. "Yes, honey, he is."

The visit to Florida was brief—barely over forty-eight hours. The following weeks blurred together with Stephanie's grief slowly softening at the edges but never loosening its grip. She moved through the house like someone trying not to wake a sleeping sorrow. She fed the kids. She answered emails. She folded laundry. But it was all mechanical, all a performance.

She found herself staring at the sky more often, not searching for signs but just wondering if anyone was listening. She didn't talk about God like she used to, not even with Matthew. The silence between her and her husband had grown quieter but not closer.

Stephanie didn't know what to do with her faith. Church had always been complicated for her. She and Matthew had baptized the kids, but they didn't go to Mass. She took issue with what the religion she was raised in had become in her mind—shame, silence, hierarchy. She had long rejected the dogma, the guilt, the way it all felt distant and cold. Except for a few weddings and Jonathan's First Communion, she hadn't been to Mass in years, even though her childhood had been shaped with rosary beads and Confession.

She had always believed in God—deeply, quietly. She loved Jesus. Even as a girl in Catholic school wearing stiff plaid skirts and reciting memorized prayers, knowing when to kneel, sit, or stand during Mass, she had felt something true behind it all. It wasn't about the rituals, the rules, or the doctrine. Underneath all that, she'd felt something alive—a whisper of divinity that had always been with her. But now, after Carmine's death, that whisper felt like a scream.

She still believed in God and somehow still loved Him beneath all her anger. But now she questioned His goodness. She was baffled by Him—by His timing, His cruelty. She couldn't fathom why God—who claimed to be love itself—would hand her a miracle and then rip it away. "What kind of God lets you live in a lie and then punishes you for learning the truth?" she asked aloud one night, standing barefoot in the hallway. She began staring at the barbershop sketch on the wall to her right as if focusing on it hard enough would undo all that had happened.

The next morning, Jonathan came into her bedroom, his eyes wide. "Mom," he said softly. "I had a dream."

Stephanie, still in bed at 10:00 a.m., barely opened her eyes. "What was it, sweetheart?"

"I saw Uncle Carmine. He was sitting under a big tree, smiling. He said he was alright. He said you don't have to be sad all the time."

Stephanie, now wide awake, stared at her son in disbelief.

"He said you're going to be okay too," Jonathan added. "He said you're stronger than you think."

Stephanie pulled Jonathan into bed and held him close, crying silently into his hair. It was the first time they'd cuddled in months.

And that's when she knew—knew that after the months of sorrow, she was craving healing. She was desperate for it, even as her anguish consumed her.

She needed something—anything. So one Sunday she slipped into a pew at St. Joseph's at the back of the sanctuary. She wore sunglasses even though it was cloudy outside. She didn't speak to anyone.

The priest talked about resurrection, about hope, about God never abandoning His children. Stephanie nearly laughed out loud.

She left before Communion, tears slipping down her cheeks as she walked briskly through the parking lot. *Such a waste of time*, she thought. She sat in her car for ten minutes before driving home.

Three nights later, while attempting to pray but not succeeding, she threw her Bible across the room in frustration. A photo of her and Carmine that she'd tucked inside fell out.

"God, where are You?" she cried. "I still believe in You. I fought to believe, but I feel abandoned. Again. Just like I felt after you took my father away. And I forgave You for that." Tears streamed down her face, her anguish swallowing her whole. "I hate you for this," she said, her voice shaking. "I hate you!"

The next morning, Maria showed up unannounced. She came with two bags—one filled with groceries and the other with a photo album containing pictures of their childhood and a framed picture of Carmine at Thanksgiving.

"Stephanie, you're still here with us. And we all love you. Please tell me how I can help you." Maria sat down beside her on the couch.

Stephanie's voice rose. "You can't help me. No one can help me. He's gone. Dead! Wrapped around a palm tree like a crumpled piece of paper. What am I supposed to do with that?"

Maria hugged her, and for the first time in weeks, Stephanie let herself be hugged. Without knowing it, she needed that hug more than anything.

A week or so later, after the kids were asleep, Stephanie lit a candle. Not a Catholic candle. Just a votive she had in the kitchen cabinet. She placed it on the buffet table in the dining room, right next to the framed picture Maria had brought, and sobbed. "I miss you so much." She sat down on a chair and pulled her knees to her chest.

Matthew came in and sat across from her. "I've been thinking about what you said," he began. "About God. I know you're angry, and I know you're suffering."

Stephanie barely looked up.

"I don't have answers," he continued. "But I don't think faith is supposed to be clean—or easy."

She stared at the flame. "It feels cruel."

"I know," he said. "But maybe it's not about understanding. Maybe it's about surviving. And having peace."

Stephanie's voice was hoarse. "I don't know how to forgive Him for this."

Matthew reached for her hand. "Then don't. Not yet. Sit with the anger. Just let it be for now."

She turned toward him. "You're not afraid I'll lose my faith?"

"No," he said. "Because I think your faith is the kind that wrestles. And that kind always finds its way back."

Stephanie's eyes filled. "I don't want to be bitter like this."

"You're not," he soothed. "You're hurt, fractured. But you're healing."

They sat in silence, the candle flickering across from them.

The next morning, Stephanie began writing. She'd always kept a journal, but she had abandoned it in her grief. She started writing other things too—letters to Carmine, scribbles in the margins of her planner, even just her brother's name on scraps of paper.

One night she wrote for over an hour. Every word was like poison leaving her soul. She wrote about rage. About God. About shame. About the Church. About the confusing space between belief and betrayal. About grief and regret. She wrote about her first phone call with Carmine. About the way he'd smiled when Gabriella handed him that crayon stick-figure family portrait. About the times when he told her he could breathe again.

When she finished, she closed the notebook and placed it on her nightstand. *I love God. I can't hate Him, but I don't understand Him*, she thought. *I want to forgive, but I don't know how. I'm still here, but barely. What's the purpose of all this?*

She found herself pulling out the photo albums once again. This time she wasn't looking for memories. She was looking for truth. She needed truth in her life but questioned what "the truth" really was.

She flipped through photos of her childhood with new eyes. The birthday parties. The dance recitals. The carefully curated family holidays. All a paradox when held against her brother's life.

Her family—all of them, the whole extended group—had loved her, yes, but they had also kept something sacred from her—something vital. How was she supposed to forget that?

She turned a page in the album she was holding and stopped at a photo of herself at age ten. She was kneeling in the grass, her eyes too old for her young face. "I always knew," she said, staring into the eyes in the picture. Then she asked aloud, "How will I get through this? I have to be okay for the kids, for Matthew." It was the first time in a long time that she'd thought of anything—anyone—other than her own grief.

The days got a little easier. Stephanie was still mostly on autopilot, but there were moments where she could forget her mourning—just for an instant. There were moments when she could again connect with her kids, with Matthew.

It was a Friday night when she sat down with Angelina. They'd spoken only brief, curt words since their big fight, but they didn't yell at each other now. They sat on the couch, hands folded, the grief still sitting heavily between them.

"I was wrong," Angelina said quietly but firmly, "to keep it from you. And I'm so sorry."

Stephanie gasped, holding back a sudden wave of tears. In that moment as she looked at her mother, she saw a broken-down old woman full of regret.

They sat in tense silence for a long time. Eventually Stephanie said, "I'm still your daughter."

Angelina took her hand. "I hope so."

They stayed together until it was time to put Gabriella to bed. They held hands in a silence that was now comforting.

Upstairs, Stephanie kissed her daughter's forehead as she tucked her in.

"Do you think Uncle Carmine is an angel now?" Gabriella asked sleepily.

Stephanie grinned. "I don't know," she said. "But I have to believe he's in Heaven."

"Even though you're mad at God?" Gabriella asked, her little voice full of wonder.

Stephanie nodded. "Even though."

Matthew peeked in from the doorway. "Are you okay?"

Stephanie shook her head slowly. "No, but I think I'm getting there."

He walked over, sat beside her, and wrapped his arms around her.

For the first time in many months, she leaned into his touch.

CHAPTER 15:

LETTERS IN VELVET (2008)

The package arrived on a Tuesday morning. Stephanie wasn't expecting a delivery—no birthdays were approaching, she hadn't placed any Home Shopping Network orders, and she hadn't bought anything online.

"Mom, there's something at the door!" Gabriella called from the living room, her voice bouncing off the walls like a ping-pong ball.

Stephanie padded over in bare feet, wiping her hands on a dish towel. Her heart gave a strange flutter as she reached for the neatly taped box. Her name was written on the address label in a slanting cursive she didn't recognize. The return address was in Fort Lauderdale, and the package was from J. Mancini.

A sense of recognition stirred within Stephanie before her mind could catch up. Florida, J—Jennifer. Carmine's cousin.

She barely knew Jennifer or her sister Cassandra outside of Carmine's few mentions of them. She hadn't seen either of them since his funeral, not since the tears and trembling hugs and the earnest, soft words: "He loved you so much, Stephanie."

"Are you gonna open it?" Gabriella asked, her hands on her hips like a miniature drill sergeant. Her school backpack was slung over one shoulder, but her stance said she wasn't going anywhere until she got an answer.

"In a few minutes," Stephanie murmured. She didn't want to tear into the package. Something about the weight of it in her hands told her this wasn't just a gift or a keepsake. The box felt much heavier than cardboard and tape, and she wanted to hang onto that feeling. "We have to get going. Let's go before you two are late for school."

Jonathan wandered in, his headphones dangling around his neck. "What's in the box?"

"I'm not sure yet," Stephanie said, trying to sound dismissive. "Go get in the car." She moved the box from the living room to the dining room table to the kitchen counter, telling herself she'd open it after dropping off the kids, after coffee, after cleaning the house, after she felt ready.

When she returned home, she sat at the kitchen table, coffee in hand. Matthew was at work, and the house was blessedly quiet. A beam of morning sunlight caught the edge of the box as she got a pair of scissors. No cleaning this morning. She sat in front of the box as if it were an altar, and she slid a scissor blade beneath the tape.

Underneath the first flap was a letter that had been carefully placed on top. Stephanie unfolded it slowly.

Stephanie,

I hope this reaches you safely.

We found this while clearing out the attic. It had been hidden away inside an old trunk, buried underneath some linens that hadn't seen light in decades. It belonged to your mother, and I knew immediately it was meant for you. We assume Victor, Cecilia's partner at the time of her death, sent it to my mother along with her ashes.

I hope it brings you something good.

With love,
Your cousin Jennifer

Stephanie's hands trembled. "Cecilia," she said aloud.

The name still felt foreign, like a character in someone else's story. This was the woman Carmine had been raised by, lived with, and suffered under—a woman Stephanie had never met.

Deeper inside the box was crumpled newspaper and some neat tissue paper. Nestled within it like something sacred was a blue velvet jewelry box. Not new. The velvet was faded, and the hinges were dulled with time.

Stephanie's breath caught. It was the jewelry box Carmine had described to her once before—the one he remembered sitting on Cecilia's dresser when he was a boy. The one he never dared to touch.

Stephanie opened it almost reverently, the hinges creaking slightly as her chest tightened. A strange, hot pressure of memory, sorrow, and anticipation filled her gut.

Inside were some hairpins, a few small black-and-white pictures—a girl growing into a woman—a Saint Christopher medal, and a silver locket. There was also a small stack of folded papers, yellowed and soft at the creases. They were tied together with a ribbon that had long lost its color.

Stephanie pulled out the first letter carefully, thinking it might disintegrate in her hand. She unfolded the paper, feeling as if she were opening up the past. Her heart clenched.

The letter was written in black ink, the handwriting delicate, loopy, and unmistakably feminine. The letter was dated May 1967.

> *To my daughter. My baby girl, Carol Ann,*
>
> *They didn't let me hold you. They said it was better that way. That it would hurt less if I didn't see your face or feel your skin against mine. They were wrong. God, they were so wrong. I didn't get to say goodbye. They wouldn't even let me give you a name, but in my heart, you are Carol Ann. I say it when no one is around. I say it when I cry into my pillow at night, hoping it echoes through time and somehow reaches you.*
>
> *They told me it was for the best. That you'd have a better life. That you'd go to a real family, not to an unwed mother like me. They said I was too young, too wrong. They didn't ask me what I wanted. It*

wasn't my choice . . . it never was. My parents were ashamed, and they said I would ruin our family name if I kept you. My boyfriend vanished after my father threatened him.

I had no one left but Linda, my twin sister, and even she couldn't stop them. We were just two stupid, scared girls who used to dream about moving to California, joining the circus, or doing anything but staying in Brooklyn.

I've tried to pretend. I've tried to forget. I've tried to move on. But how could I ever forget you? You are with me in every breath, and I see you everywhere. Every baby girl I pass on the street, I wonder if it could be you. Every time I go by the hospital where you were born, my knees go weak.

A month after they took you, Linda and I heard from Mrs. Rossellini down the block that a couple on Cropsey Avenue just had a baby girl. Word spreads fast around here, and I was told that people were shocked because the couple had been married for a decade yet never had any children. Someone told me they were showing her off like a prized trophy, walking her around in a new white carriage with pink trim.

As soon as I heard that, I snapped. I dragged Linda out of bed the next morning, and we spent that entire Saturday combing every square inch of Bensonhurst. Like two crazy women, we looked into carriages and peeked into laundromats. We watched women in markets and on corners, hoping we'd see a baby with your eyes. Linda said your eyes were big and brown, almond-shaped, just like ours are. We hoped that by some miracle we would find you.

I thought I saw you once—this baby with brown curls and socks with lace. I started crying right there on the sidewalk. Linda put her arms around me, and we just sat on the curb until the streetlights came on.

We never found out who that baby was. We were just two girls trying to chase a ghost in baby shoes.

I know I messed up. I know I'll never get to raise you or kiss your scraped knees or braid your hair before school. But I want you to know I will never forget you. I will never stop loving you. Not for a second.

I hope you're happy. I hope you're safe. I hope they love you the way I want to. Wherever you are, I hope someone is kissing you goodnight.

With all the love I'll never get to give,
Your Mommy

Stephanie sat frozen, her fingers clutching the edge of the paper. She didn't realize she was crying until a teardrop fell onto the page, smudging the ink slightly. She pressed her fingers to her lips, inhaling sharply. Her birth mother's voice had come alive through the paper—ragged, raw, and unapologetically grieving.

She stared at the name Cecilia had given her: Carol Ann. Not Stephanie. Not the name on her driver's license, phone bill, or credit cards. Not the name she knew herself by but another name—her first given name.

For the first time in her life, Stephanie had a glimpse into the heart of the woman who had given her life. The ache of it was almost unbearable. She read the letter again, more slowly this time, her fingertips brushing every loop of Cecilia's pen. Her heart throbbed with something too complicated to name—grief maybe. Or relief. Or both.

Looking at the next letter, she hesitated, unsure whether she was ready to read what came next. There had to be at least a dozen letters in total, each one her birth mother's voice reaching through the years, each one a window into Cecilia's life.

The next letter was dated November 1972.

Dear Carol Ann,

I don't know where you are. I don't know if you're still in Brooklyn or if your new family moved you somewhere nicer. But I write anyway. I write because I need to say your name out loud, even if only on paper.

I had another baby right after you were born. Same father. It was a boy, and his name is Carmine.

He's you in ways I can't explain. Linda says he has the same eyes, and the same stubborn little chin, as you. Sometimes when he laughs, I hear a voice I've never known but I've always imagined. It's your voice, hidden inside his joy. I feel like you're connected somehow. Like you're both pieces of me that got scattered in different directions.

James—my boyfriend and your father—married me before Carmine was born. I think he wanted to make things right. He convinced himself that he loved me, or maybe he thought love could grow from guilt. But we were doomed before we began. I left him when Carmine was only a few months old.

I'm not raising Carmine alone, not really. My parents help a lot, and we live with them. Linda too. God bless her—she's still my anchor, even when I drift. We take turns with meals and baths and goodnight songs. Sometimes I watch my mother—your nonna, Concetta—read him bedtime stories, and I wonder if she ever thinks about you. She never mentions you, and neither does my father, Leo. It's like you were erased. But I remember. I always remember.

Carmine doesn't know about you. I can't tell him, and I don't know if I ever will. He's only four years old now, and he deserves a clean slate. He deserves joy without shadows.

But I imagine I can see you in him. In the way he curls his fingers around mine. In the way he looks at me like he's trying to understand something I haven't said. I wonder if you do that too, if you have that same quiet curiosity.

I try to be a good mother. I do. But some days I fail him, and I know it. Like I'm too damaged to give him what he needs. Yet I love Carmine. And really, I try. I smile when I'm supposed to. I sing songs. I pack his preschool lunches. When I kiss his forehead, I mean it. But inside, I'm still grieving you. And I hate that he has to grow up with that kind of silence in the room.

I love you. I love you two in different ways, but both bottomlessly.

With all my heart,
Your mom,
Cecilia

Stephanie read the next few letters in succession. The handwriting grew shakier, the paper thinner, the tone more fragmented. Cecilia's voice shifted—from a young mother drowning in guilt to a woman descending into mental illness. Mentions of Carmine became less frequent. They were replaced by references to long nights and restless thoughts.

The letters thinned out after 1978, as if life had swallowed Cecilia whole. Then after a long pause came one letter—the last letter—dated November 1984. Stephanie unfolded it carefully, bracing herself.

Dear daughter,

The breeze here in Hawaii smells like salt and coconut and everything I never had growing up in Brooklyn. Victor, my partner who moved me here, is inside cooking something that smells like garlic and onions, as usual. The sun is setting in gold and pink, and the sky looks like it's been painted by someone who knows exactly what beauty is supposed to look like.

But I don't feel beautiful tonight. I feel hollow.

I have lung cancer. It's very advanced, and the doctors say there's nothing they can do for me. I feel like one of those old ashtrays I used to keep on the kitchen table, all burned through and cracked.

They don't know how long I have, but I can feel the clock ticking inside me. It will be soon, that I know.

I thought I should spend my last days doing something risky or dramatic. Maybe climb a mountain or jump out of a plane. But all I want is you. All I've ever wanted is you.

You're the ghost I've lived with since I was eighteen years old. The ache that never went away. It's been seventeen years of aching, of missing you.

When the doctors diagnosed me, I drove to the edge of the island and screamed your name into the ocean. I hope somehow the waves carried it to you.

Victor doesn't know I'm writing this. He doesn't ask many questions. Maybe that's why I picked him. He's a mechanic, loud and hot-tempered. He drinks and smokes too much. He yells sometimes. But he's never asked me about you because I never told him about you. And somehow that makes things easier.

Victor isn't perfect, but I spent so many years with men who wanted to fix me when I was unfixable. I still am, probably, yet he loves me just enough. He takes care of me in his own way.

I've told you how I lived after you were born. Every chance I got, I was in a bar with the type of friends who aren't really friends. I went through more men than I can count. I used everything I could to get through each day, from pills to vodka. I exploited anything that dulled the part of me that loves you, that has regret. None of it helped, not really. The only thing that could help is you.

I never told your brother about you. Carmine is a teenager now, but he's still just a boy. I don't want to ruin him with my sadness. I left him back in Brooklyn to shield him from that sorrow. It was destroying him. I could see it.

He always knew something was wrong with me, that something was missing from his life. He carried that pain, and it nearly killed me. And now I'll never get to see you both together. That's the part that hurts the most. I hope that somehow, someway, you find each other someday.

I used to think love was something you had to chase, or earn, or drink away when it didn't come. But now, with the clock ticking louder every day, I've started to believe something else.

Now I believe that God was with me, even in the mess. Even in the numbing. Even in the years when I tried to disappear and cauterize the wounds.

I don't know how to explain it, but I feel God now. He's in the breeze, in the sunset, in the aching that's defined me for so long. I think He's the one who kept your name alive in me. I wish I had more time to learn about Him, to build my trust in Him.

I want you to know that if you ever feel lost, or broken, or like you're too far gone to be found . . . you're not.

God is the answer to everything I couldn't fix. I hope you find Him. I hope He finds you.

And I hope you know that love—real love—is never wasted. Not even when it's buried under years of silence and distance.

I hope you don't hate me. I hope you can forgive me. For years I hated the girl I saw in the mirror, the one who gave away her baby. I never forgave her. Maybe you will. And I hope you understand. I love you.

Forever and always,
Your birth mother,
Cecilia

Stephanie closed her eyes. She'd been reading for an hour, and now the words blurred, swimming behind her eyelids. A vision bloomed in her mind: Cecilia barefoot on a Hawaiian beach, coughing into her palm, salt in her hair and grief in her lungs, writing furiously as if the letters could carry her sins away on paper wings.

Stephanie folded the last letter, her entire body buzzing. Her heart, heavy and raw, thumped like it wanted to break free from her chest.

She sat in silence for a long time, the jewelry box still open beside her, the scent of old paper and musty velvet rising from it.

She felt like cracked glass—fractured, but catching light in new places.

This woman—her birth mother—was no longer a myth, not a shadow. She had a voice, a face, a heart. And that heart had broken every day since 1967.

She imagined Cecilia writing these letters in secret, each word a thread in a tapestry Stephanie hadn't known she was part of, and then hiding them away in a box only her daughter was ever meant to find.

Still crying, Stephanie reached for her journal and opened a fresh page. With her pen cocked between her fingers, she hovered over the blank page, unsure of where to begin. The pen felt heavier than usual, like it carried the weight of two lifetimes.

She didn't know what she was about to write, only that she had to write something. Maybe for herself. Maybe for Cecilia. Maybe for the little girl in the white stroller with pink trim on Cropsey Avenue.

She put the pen to the page and wrote her first few words. She felt they would be the beginning of something new. Something hopeful.

CHAPTER 16:
ORPHANED AGAIN
(2009)

Stephanie kept writing in her journal every day—sometimes about Carmine, sometimes about Cecilia, sometimes about just how difficult it was to make it through the day without her brother. Cecilia's letters had sparked a bevy of new questions in her head and heart, and with Carmine and the rest of his family passed, she could only imagine—in stories that were hazy, smudged around the edges, and compiled from what little she knew of Cecilia—what her birth mother was like. It made her value Angelina that much more, despite the secrets she'd kept.

Stephanie's relationship with Angelina had softened over the last year. What was done was done, and life didn't come with do-overs. She made a conscious effort to bicker with her mother less, use a calmer tone when she spoke to her, and give her space without being distant. Angelina, though set in her ways, did the same.

The chest pains started on a Thursday in early January. Angelina had just finished folding the towels, humming along to Glenn Miller's "Stardust" as Stephanie was rinsing out the mugs of coffee that had gone cold hours ago.

When the sharpness hit, like a fist clenching inside her chest, Angelina was forced to sit down. Stephanie, hearing her mother's gasp, rushed into the living room, but Angelina waved her daughter away. She waited for the sensation to pass and then chalked it up to indigestion. Too much sausage bread and pastries over the holidays, she claimed. After all, Christmas had been indulgent, with New Year's even worse. Even still, Stephanie insisted that Angelina call her doctor.

When Angelina's doctor called back, he agreed with Angelina. "You're eighty-four," he said with a chuckle. "Your heart's fine, and your last EKG was normal. It's probably just the tomato sauce fighting back. Take it easy, and cut back on heavy foods."

Stephanie wasn't convinced, but there was little else she could do.

That evening, Stephanie started sorting through the mail that she hadn't gotten to earlier in the day. The Glenn Miller record had long stopped spinning, but the silence felt louder than the music ever had. Matthew walked in from work, his tie loosened and sleeves rolled up, sensing something was wrong.

"She's not okay," Stephanie said immediately, not turning around. "I know Mom says it's indigestion, but it's not. I saw her collapse into her recliner this afternoon like gravity had doubled. I'm scared."

Matthew moved closer, resting his hand on the table. "Start at the beginning."

Stephanie told him about the afternoon. "I know her. I know her body language. She's hiding something."

Matthew nodded, serious. "Do you want me to come with you? To the hospital?"

Stephanie tore up a piece of junk mail with a firm finality. "I think I need to take her tonight. No waiting. I just needed to say it out loud first . . . to someone who won't tell me I'm overreacting."

"You're not," he said. "You're doing what she'd do for you."

Just then, Angelina's voice floated in from the living room, raspy but firm. "I heard that."

Stephanie stepped into the doorway. "Then you know I'm serious."

Angelina was sitting upright on the couch, her arms crossed, her face pale but defiant. "I'm not going to the hospital tonight. I've had agita before. I'll take another antacid. I'll sleep it off."

"You nearly fainted earlier."

"I sat down too fast. That's all."

Stephanie moved closer, her voice low but steady. "Mom, I saw your hand shaking when you reached for that glass. You winced when you stood. This isn't just indigestion."

Angelina's eyes narrowed. "You're making it into something it's not. I'm tired, not dying."

Matthew lingered in the kitchen, listening.

Stephanie kneeled beside her mother. "Mom, I'm trying to protect you. Please."

Angelina looked away, her jaw clenched. "Hospitals keep you overnight for nothing. I'm not going."

Stephanie's voice cracked. "You're scared."

Angelina's gaze snapped onto Stephanie's eyes. "No, I'm angry. My own daughter doesn't trust me. I know my own body."

Stephanie swallowed hard. "I trust you. But I also know you. And I know when you're bluffing."

A long silence stretched between them. Then Angelina sighed, her shoulders sagging. "Tomorrow, if I still feel off, we'll go."

Stephanie nodded, but her eyes didn't soften. "I'm holding you to that."

Angelina turned toward the window, watching the night settle in. She stayed that way until Stephanie and Matthew went up to bed.

The next morning, after Stephanie dropped the kids off at school, Angelina shuffled into the kitchen in her slippers and robe, pressing her hand against her chest.

Stephanie looked up from the table. "You okay, Mom?"

Angelina waved her off. "It's nothing. I ate too many stuffed artichokes on New Year's Day. My stomach is doing cartwheels."

Stephanie didn't like the way her mother looked—pale around the mouth, a shine of sweat along her forehead. "Let me call the doctor again," she said.

"Oh stop, I'm fine," Angelina snapped, brushing past her to grab a napkin.

The pains continued off and on throughout the day, and Angelina refused to go to the hospital again and again. She had nothing but ginger ale and crackers all day, and she finished all the antacids in the house, but nothing really helped. By the time Stephanie went to pick up the kids, she was at the end of her rope and afraid to leave her mother alone for even a half hour.

That night, Stephanie found Angelina sitting on the edge of her bed, hunched over, her hands shaking, her face a sickly shade of gray. "We're going to the hospital, Mom," she said. "No arguments, no discussion."

Angelina tried to smile, but it collapsed halfway. "I just need a minute."

Stephanie grabbed her keys and purse, helped her mother into the car, and sped toward the hospital, her heart pounding louder than the engine's roar. By the time they reached Ocean University Medical Center, Angelina was having a heart attack.

Everything in the ER blurred—shouts, monitors, nurses rushing. Stephanie stood frozen as they wheeled her mother away, the words *emergency stent* and *no prior history* ringing in her ears.

They told her Angelina had suffered a massive myocardial infarction. It was a blockage—the kind that kills quickly if not caught in time. The news hit Stephanie like a brick to her stomach. She called Matthew and told him she wouldn't be home anytime soon.

"She's stable," the surgeon said an hour later, pulling off his cap and gloves. "We inserted the stent. She made it through the operation, but her body is weak. At her age, recovery is often difficult. She will also need another procedure, but we must wait for her to get stronger. The next few days are critical."

After the hospital staff found Angelina a room, Stephanie sat at her mother's bedside, staring at the machines, the tubes, the IVs, and the metal bed rails. She reached for her mother's hand, and in her softest voice, her pleading voice, she said, "I need you to wake up. I need you to be okay. Please, Mom."

Angelina stirred just enough to squeeze her daughter's fingers.

A day passed, then two, then three, with Stephanie constantly at her mother's side. She brought books, flowers, Gabriella's drawings, anything to cheer up Angelina. But mostly Stephanie brought herself—raw and still carrying so many questions.

By the fifth afternoon, as the winter sun slatted through the blinds, Angelina was strong enough for her breathing tube to be removed. Now she could speak, though her voice was hoarse. Her hair was flattened on one side, and her face was drawn, but her eyes were clearer than they'd been in months.

"You look awful, sweetheart," Angelina croaked. "You don't have to stay all day, you know."

Stephanie laughed through her tears. "You're one to talk. And I want to." She brushed a strand of hair from her mother's temple. "I've been praying every day."

Angelina turned her head slowly. "Me too. I asked God to give me one more chance. One more chance to make things right."

Their eyes met, and for a moment, the machines faded away.

"I think He heard you." Stephanie leaned in closer. "Do you think God forgives us before we ask?"

Angelina's voice was faint. "I think He knows our hearts. Even the parts we hide."

Stephanie nodded, tears catching in her throat. "He knows I need to hear it from you."

"And I need to say it. In the way you need to hear it." Angelina reached for her daughter's hand. "I should've told you years ago," she said. "I was a coward—I just couldn't bear the thought of you not being mine. Every day I pray you truly forgive me."

"I was always yours. Even when I didn't know, even after I found out." Stephanie's voice broke. "You're my mother, and I forgive you."

They cried together. Not loudly. Just enough to let go of the pain and let the wall between them dissolve.

Angelina remained in the hospital for well over a week. On the eleventh day, after Stephanie had promised Gabriella that she would volunteer at the school's annual book fair, Stephanie told her mother she would be gone for a bit. "Just an hour," she insisted. "I'll come right back."

"Go. Life doesn't wait," Angelina said brightly.

Stephanie kissed her mother's forehead and left her bundled in a knit blanket by the window. She hated to admit it, but she knew a little while away from her mother's bedside would probably do her some good.

The book fair was in full swing when Stephanie arrived. Gabriella had collected a stack of books half as tall as she was, and she proudly showed them off at her mother's table.

Not thirty minutes later, Stephanie's phone buzzed in her back pocket. She didn't recognize the number but headed into the hallway and took the call anyway.

Code blue, they said. They were trying to revive her. The nurse told Stephanie to come right away.

Stephanie didn't remember driving to the hospital. It felt as if she was suddenly just standing there outside her mother's room, talking to the medical staff as they were going in and out trying to save her mother. Someone asked if Angelina had a DNR. Everything was happening too quickly, and then, as fast as it happened, Stephanie found herself alone with her mother. She held her hand, listening to the slowing beeps of the machines.

Stephanie blinked against the light, bowed her head, clasped her hands, and began saying the Lord's Prayer. She let the silence settle for a bit and then added, "God, if You're listening, take her gently. She's tired, but she's loved. Bless her with forgiveness for any wrongs she carried. And forgive me for the hurt I caused in return."

Only moments later, the machines slowed to almost nothing, and Stephanie felt her mother's hand grow still in hers.

"Fly free, Mom," she whispered. "Go dance with Daddy. Give Carmine a kiss, and thank the woman who gave me life."

Stephanie sat quietly. She simply held her mother's hand and listened to the nothingness, imagining Angelina's soul rising—light as breath—into the arms of God. She pictured her father, Jack, waiting there, patient as ever, his hand outstretched, the years between them folding into nothing.

Stephanie stayed until the sun began to set, her hand still entwined with Angelina's, the hush of Heaven in the air.

A nurse came into the room. "She's gone, Stephanie," she said respectfully, not as an announcement but as a benediction. "She waited for you."

Stephanie drove away from the hospital in silence, the kind that pressed against the windows and settled in her chest. The streets passed by—bare trees, salt-streaked pavement, the occasional flicker of porch lights—but she barely saw any of it. Her hands gripped the wheel, her knuckles pale, the scent of the hospital still lingering on her skin, her clothes, and the folded blanket in the passenger seat.

She drove, the tears not yet coming, as if the motion of the car could hold her together. Eleven days in the hospital. Eleven days of prayers and bedside confessions. Eleven last days with her mother.

At home, Stephanie stepped inside and stood for a moment in the doorway, unsure where to place the weight of Angelina's absence. It was late, far too late to wake Matthew or the kids. She crossed the living room and laid the blanket across the armchair—carefully, reverently, its yarn still steeped in antiseptic and memory. "I'll keep you right here, Mom," she said, talking into the empty room, grateful they'd had the chance for forgiveness.

∞ ∞ ∞

The morning after the funeral, with grief still clinging to her like damp clothes, Stephanie sat at her desk and typed a name she'd barely dared to speak aloud: James Esposito. Then she typed into the search bar every small detail she knew about her birth father—lived in Brooklyn; married to Cecilia Russo; now in Florida. She expected no results. Instead, the screen blinked back at her with an address on Michigan Isle Road in Lake Worth, Florida. With so little information, a stranger's life had been mapped and numbered. Her own origin was suddenly traceable.

Stephanie didn't want anything from James. She already had a father—one who was gone too soon but had adored her, who'd shown up for every scraped knee, who'd cuddled her to sleep at night. But something in her had stirred: She had four parents, and with James the only one surviving, an indefinable urgency had crept into her soul. It was an urgency to tell the man who'd vanished that his first-born child had lived a full, complicated life—to tell him that Carmine was gone.

She didn't know if James would want to know any of it or if he would even care. Still, with the memory of the funeral still foremost in her mind, writing to him felt like the one thing she could do to make peace with the vacuum he'd left behind.

She pulled out a sheet of lined paper. Once she started writing, she couldn't stop. Childhood memories spilled out, some tender, some jagged. Every detail she could remember about her life flowed out of her like an endless wave. It felt good, cathartic. She wrote until her hand cramped, until the ink blurred from her tears. Before she knew it, she'd written four pages—four pages of truth folded into an envelope like a prayer.

She sent it by certified mail, return receipt requested, just to ensure its delivery. She didn't expect a reply or even necessarily want one. She just wanted the echo of her words to land in a part of her past she never knew, somewhere beyond herself. She yearned for this door to close somehow.

The next few weeks went slowly, with Angelina's absence everywhere in the house and the grief too fresh. Stephanie wrote every day: letters to her mother, letters to Carmine, letters to God. Then she wrote letters to the version of herself that had believed in goodness. She folded each one up and tucked them away in her dresser drawer, grasping at the fragile threads of healing, hoping one might hold.

She started sitting on the back porch in the evenings, usually wrapped in Carmine's sweatshirt, just to find some comfort. *I've lost so many people*, she thought. *And I don't know how I'll ever make it without Mom.*

Months after Angelina's death, Stephanie received a letter from James. Stunned, she was slightly afraid to open it. The kids were in school, and Matthew was at work, so in the silence of the day, she began to read.

Dear Stephanie,

I'm sorry to hear about Carmine. The few times I met him, he always struck me as a complicated young man. I think he was searching for something.

He came to see me years ago, but it didn't go well. He wanted information I didn't have. He mentioned you and said he'd only recently learned he had a sister. I tried to be careful with what I said because I didn't want to tarnish his view of his mother, but I really didn't have much to offer him. Cecilia's parents hadn't wanted me around once they found out she was pregnant, and they'd handled everything back then. I couldn't give him what he wanted.

My time with Cecilia was brief—maybe two years, all told. It was the late sixties, a wild time. I was married to another woman when we first met, and things weren't exactly monogamous on either side. Cecilia was part of the fallout.

I'm not telling you this to cast judgment on Cecilia. Believe me, I wasn't a saint. Lots of drinking, lots of girlfriends, lots of fights. No drugs, though; I was never into that stuff.

Cecilia and I crossed paths again later. We married briefly. That's when we had Carmine, but she left me right after that. Her parents got the marriage annulled almost immediately. In the short time I knew Cecilia, I visited her house only once. I wasn't exactly welcomed.

I'm glad to hear about your adoptive parents. They chose you, raised you, and loved you. It's nice to know they were Italian, and it sounds like you cherished them. It's honorable that you took care of your mother in her golden years.

You seem to have built a beautiful life. It sounds like you have a good marriage, nice children, and lots of stability. That's more than most can say.

I wish you continued happiness.

Best,
James

It was obvious that James wanted no further contact. And that was fine with Stephanie. The letter was so carefully constructed that it didn't bring her the peace that she needed, just proof—proof that she hadn't imagined him wrong. James was exactly who Carmine said he was: cold-hearted, disconnected, and unable to take responsibility for his actions.

Stephanie folded the letter and placed it in the drawer with the others, feeling as though she should have left things well enough alone. She closed the drawer with a thump. Then she opened it again and stared at the stack. Each letter was a failed attempt at closure. Then she pulled James's letter out and placed it at the bottom—not erased, just buried. She would decide later if it deserved to stay. *Some doors don't close; they stay ajar with what might've been*, she said to herself.

She didn't cry after reading James's letter. Not right away. She just sat there feeling the weight of everything unsaid. It was strange how something so meticulously worded could still feel like abandonment, like being erased politely.

That night she lay awake listening to the wind against the windows, wondering if healing was just another word for forgetting. She didn't want to forget, but she couldn't live like this either.

CHAPTER 17:

Old Streets, Fresh Eyes (2009)

Stephanie sat cross-legged on her bedroom floor with a faded map of Brooklyn spread out before her. It was creased and fragile from years of being folded away and forgotten. Jonathan kneeled beside her, tracing his finger over the faded map with curious eyes.

"Where's Bensonhurst?" her son asked.

Stephanie pointed to a familiar section of the map. "You don't remember because you were younger. Right there, baby. That's where Mommy grew up." Then she traced a line with her index finger to a nearby area. "You were born there."

Jonathan blinked up at her. "Is that where Uncle Carmine grew up too?"

Stephanie's throat tightened. "Yes. He lived in this part of Bensonhurst," she said, pointing. "And I," she moved her finger slightly, "lived in this part."

"You were neighbors?" Jonathan asked, his eyes widening.

"Almost, sweetie. All those years we were so close, and we didn't even know it."

Matthew appeared in the doorway with his suitcase in hand. "Jonathan, why don't you go pick out two DVDs to bring with us?"

Jonathan's eyes lit up. "Really? One for the way there, and one for the way back?"

Matthew laughed. "Yes. Quick, before I change my mind."

Jonathan ran out of the room in a burst of energy. "Gabby, we can take two movies!" he cried at the top of his lungs.

Matthew crouched down next to his wife. "I'm so glad you agreed to do this. Maybe it'll help you get your energy back."

Stephanie sighed, acknowledging that there were still too many days when it was simply too hard to get out of bed. She didn't want to be like this, but nothing was really helping.

She nodded. "I need to do this. For him. For Mom. For me. For all of us. And it's just Brooklyn. It's not like we're going into Manhattan. It won't be too overwhelming."

They packed sparingly, with snacks, light jackets, and some favorite CDs for the ride. They were spending just one night in Brooklyn. It would be enough time to walk the streets, breathe in the salt-kissed air of Coney Island, and let the children see the place that shaped their mom, their mom's mom, and—unknowingly—their uncle too.

It was early when they wrangled the kids into the car. Matthew drove the ninety minutes into Brooklyn. The kids squabbled over song choices as they went, but Stephanie just stared out the window, her eyes welling up, watching the city rise up like a memory. "Everyone I've ever loved is from Brooklyn," she said, sobbing lightly, "including Carmine."

The Verrazano Bridge loomed in the distance as their car made its way down the Staten Island Expressway. Stephanie leaned her forehead against the glass, watching as the skyline shifted and the borough of her youth drew closer. She hadn't been back in years—not since the last of her family's gatherings dwindled away and the neighborhood had begun to change.

As they pulled onto Bay Parkway, a wave of nostalgia hit her so hard that she had to steady her breathing. "There used to be a pastry shop right there," Stephanie said, pointing out the window to a shuttered storefront. She turned to face the kids. "My mom would take me there after Sunday Mass for warm zeppole and hot chocolate."

Gabriella looked up from her Game Boy. "What's a zeppole?"

Stephanie laughed. "It's a magical ball of fried dough covered in powdered sugar. You'll see."

They drove for a few more minutes, and then Matthew pulled up to the curb in front of Cropsey Park. Stephanie stepped out of the car slowly, shielding her eyes against the high spring sun. The park was just as she remembered, with bouncing basketballs and shrieking children. Her kids briefly stopped to watch the older men playing chess while Matthew walked over to the racquetball court, remembering how he and his buddies often played handball.

Then Stephanie led the kids toward the playground. She noticed the budding branches on the trees and heard the distant rumble of the B6 city bus. The weather was better than she could have hoped for—no storm clouds or showers. The day was beautiful with only the slightest chill.

"This is where my dad, your Grandpa Jack, used to push me on the swings," she said to the kids. "Right there. That one."

Gabriella ran to the swing and hopped on, kicking off with glee. "Push me, Mom!"

Stephanie stepped behind her and began to push, the creaking of the chains almost hypnotic.

"Did Uncle Carmine get pushed too?" Gabriella squealed.

Stephanie paused as her stomach twisted in a knot. "I'm not sure, honey." She fell silent but continued to push Gabriella higher and higher, her daughter's giggles combatting her threatening tears.

Matthew came up beside his wife, noticing the heaviness in her face. "Are you hanging in there?"

She nodded, though her chest ached. "I just keep wondering . . . about it all. Did my brother stand right here?"

Matthew squeezed her hand. "Maybe he did."

She wiped away a stray tear. "Were Mom, Dad, and I here on the swings at the same time Carmine and Cecilia were right over there on the slide? Were we all together without knowing it?"

"Maybe," Matthew answered. He gave her hand another squeeze. "But it's even more likely that they weren't. You will never know, so please, honey, don't torture yourself. We're here now, together." He gave a half-smile that felt comforting, reassuring.

When the kids had their fill of the park, the four of them drove a few blocks and stopped outside a red brick building—Lafayette High School. It looked tired but was still standing strong. Stephanie stood on the sidewalk and stared up at it, her mind absorbed by the memories.

"That's your old school?" Jonathan asked.

"Yup," she replied. "It was big and chaotic, and I used to dream of dancing on a real stage one day. I never got the chance, though, since life had other plans for me."

Gabriella tilted her head. "Like what?"

Stephanie smiled sadly. "Like being there for my mom, your nana. And now, for you." She pointed to the steps where she used to sit with her Walkman and dream of auditions and Broadway lights. "I used to practice my dancing for hours, and I tried out for every dance team and musical. I thought I would be famous," she said, half laughing.

"You are," Gabriella said, grinning. "To us."

Stephanie's smile grew, her heart aching in the best way.

"Uncle Carmine went to this high school too," Stephanie said, almost to herself.

Gabriella jumped right into her question. "But if you were here . . . and Uncle Carmine was here . . . how come you didn't know each other?"

Stephanie swallowed. "It was a school with thousands of kids. And grown-ups made choices they thought were right. Those choices kept us apart."

Gabriella pouted. "Grown-ups are always making choices for kids."

"Grown-ups do what they think is right," Stephanie replied in her best mom voice. "But never mind that. I have somewhere else to show you, somewhere fun."

They reached Coney Island in mid-afternoon. The boardwalk was just coming alive for the start of the season. Most of the rides weren't open yet, but the Wonder Wheel stood tall, defiant against the blue sky.

Stephanie stood still as the ocean breeze tangled her hair. She closed her eyes and listened—to the waves, to the memories.

"We were supposed to come here together," she said to Matthew. "Carmine wanted to see it all again, to ride the Cyclone like when we were kids, to eat at Nathan's and watch the fireworks."

Matthew wrapped an arm around her. "He's here, Steph. Maybe not how you wanted, but he's here."

They got Nathan's famous hot dogs and then walked across the boardwalk and onto the sand where Stephanie laid out a big beach blanket. After they ate, Stephanie and Matthew watched as Jonathan wrote his name in the sand and Gabriella chased seagulls.

On their boardwalk stroll back, Stephanie pointed out the arcade where she used to trade in winning game tickets for prizes and penny candy. The photo booth where she'd had her first kiss was still there.

They found the zeppole stand with its faded awning just where she remembered it, beside the boardwalk's rusted coin-op binoculars. The little balls of dough tasted like childhood—sweet, ephemeral, and just a little too hot to hold. The kids loved them, leaving powdered sugar wisping behind them like a breadcrumb trail to the past. Stephanie remembered with a sigh that zeppole from this stand were her mother's favorite.

From there, it was merely steps to the amusement park—Luna Park. At the game booths, Matthew won the kids stuffed animals. Gabriella screamed on the kiddie-coaster, and Jonathan laughed with that same crooked grin Carmine had in the one photo Stephanie couldn't stop staring at. She laughed for the first time in months. She felt almost like herself again.

After a ten-minute drive, they parked across from Saint Finbar Catholic Church, its bell tower casting a long shadow over Bay 20th Street, its old stone facade as impressive as ever. The kids tumbled out of the car, their hands still sticky from the zeppole they'd eaten, their sneakers slapping against the pavement.

"This is where I used to go to church," Stephanie said, her voice softer than she expected, "every Sunday, rain or shine. Your Grandpa Jack would wear the same brown sports jacket to Mass every week, even in July."

The children looked up at the building, unimpressed by its age but curious about their mother's tone. The church doors were closed, but the stained glass glowed faintly in the afternoon light—Saint Francis cradling a lamb and Mother Mary with her hands open.

Stephanie led them to the steps where she used to sit with her friends after Mass and watch the pigeons fight over crumbs while the adults chatted. Her fingers brushed the railing, cool and familiar.

"I used to think God lived in that ceiling," she said, pointing toward the arch above the entrance. "That if I stared long enough, He would blink." The kids laughed, but she didn't. A memory emerged: At six or seven years old, she'd said that to her mother. Angelina had chuckled kindly before explaining about God living in Heaven.

They didn't go inside. Stephanie didn't need to. The memories were enough—the echo of her mother's heels on the marble floor, the hush before Communion, the way her father would squeeze her hand during the final hymn.

As they walked back to the car, Jonathan asked, "Do you miss going there?"

Stephanie paused. "Sometimes, because this is where I first met Jesus. There are a lot of good memories here, but this place now . . . it feels like a dream I woke up from."

They got the kids back in the car for their next destination. Stephanie and Matthew had saved the best for last—the famous L&B Spumoni Gardens. Stephanie could smell the eatery before they even pulled up—the warm garlic, the crispy crusts, the sweet hint of cream.

"Best Sicilian slice in the world," she told her kids as they climbed out of the car. "And the spumoni—a special type of Italian ice cream—is homemade."

Inside, the red-checkered tablecloths and buzzing neon signs made it feel like time hadn't touched the place. They ordered a full tray of Sicilian pizza, and Jonathan devoured three slices. Gabriella licked her spumoni spoon clean. Stephanie sipped a glass of red wine, staring at the seat across from her like she expected Carmine to appear there, grinning and waving a slice in the air.

Matthew reached across the table and took Stephanie's hand. "I think this trip . . . I think he would have loved it. I think your mother would have loved it too."

Stephanie looked at him, looked at her children, and felt her past and future sitting side by side. It was as if Angelina was looking over one of her shoulders and Carmine was looking over the other.

That night, in their hotel room that overlooked the bridge, Stephanie stood at the window, watching the lights of Brooklyn twinkle like stars in the sky. She thought of how her whole life had been shaped in these few blocks. She thought of how Carmine's life had been shaped in almost the exact same blocks—blocks that might as well have been oceans apart.

Outside, the city breathed around her. She opened her journal and began to write.

Carmine,

Today I walked through your childhood without you.

I saw the swing sets we must have both played on. The pizza place you loved. The high school I dreamed my dreams in.

And I brought the kids. I tried my best to tell them stories about my life growing up and about their Nana Angelina. I trust you both have peace in Heaven.

I wish you were here. But maybe you are. Maybe this was always meant to happen this way. Maybe this was the only way.

You were taken from me, but I carry you now. In every story, in every memory, in every heartbeat.

I love you.
Stephanie

She closed the journal, held it to her chest, and let the tears fall. Her heart answered back, *Carmine is never really gone. He lives in you.*

Stephanie sat by the window and continued watching the city lights flicker. She thought about her father, Jack, gone too soon. About her mother, Angelina, who loved her intensely but imperfectly. About Carmine, the brother she barely got to know, and about her birth mother who never stopped loving her.

She thought about loss—not as an ending but as a thread woven through the fabric of life. A reminder of what mattered. Of who mattered.

She opened her journal one more time and wrote: "Loss doesn't erase love. It carves it deeper. And every scar it leaves becomes a story we carry forward."

Stephanie closed the book, gazed at her children sleeping soundly in the bed next to hers, and thanked God for another day. For this day. She turned off the lights and let the city sing her to sleep.

CHAPTER 18:

Into the Arms of Peace (2009)

Stephanie drove aimlessly around Point Pleasant, the Sunday morning sun bright with springtime. They'd returned from their Brooklyn trip yesterday, and now going straight home after running her errands felt too daunting. She had too much to think about, too much in her full but breaking heart.

The streets of the town rolled by. She drove past the school, the diner, the cemetery. And then, as always, she passed the little white chapel with the red door that sat just off Main Street, nestled between an old hardware store and a bakery that always smelled like cinnamon. Stephanie had passed the chapel a thousand times before on her way to school drop-offs, to the grocery store, to nowhere in particular. It had often caught her eye.

The red door seemed to shimmer in the sunlight, brighter than everything that surrounded it. The door looked freshly painted, almost too vibrant against the white clapboard siding and the weathered shingles above. The building was modest, almost simple. There was no towering steeple. No stained-glass windows. Just a small wooden sign that read "Grace Fellowship. Sundays at 10:00 a.m."

For years, the chapel had intrigued her, not because it was grand or famous or even particularly noticeable, but because something about it called to her softly every time she passed. She had never gone in, not even once.

She told herself she stayed away because she didn't have time. Or because organized religion wasn't her style. Or because the kids had sports. Or because she already believed in God—she didn't need a church to prove that.

But the truth was simpler. She was afraid. Afraid of being judged. Afraid of not fitting in. Afraid that stepping inside would force her to confront the many things she wasn't ready to face. It was all so different from the Catholicism she'd been raised in—and part of her was afraid to walk away from that faith.

But then came Carmine and the accident. Then the unraveling. Then her mother's passing. Then the depression. And now, nothing felt certain anymore.

Until now. Until right this moment. She turned the car around and pulled into the small gravel lot. She stared at the red door, her heart thudding. The car idled as her thoughts swirled. What if people wanted to talk to her? What if she cried? What if she didn't feel anything at all? Her fingers gripped the steering wheel as if it were a lifeline. She thought of something Carmine once said: "You don't need a cathedral to talk to God." Maybe this was what he meant.

She watched people going into the chapel—families, couples, elderly men in baseball caps, teenagers with coffee cups. Some wore jeans. One woman wore pajama pants. All were greeting each other warmly.

No one looked perfect. No one looked like they belonged to a club she couldn't join. Even still, Stephanie was about to talk herself into driving away when she noticed a sign taped to the front door: "Come as you are. All are welcome."

"All are welcome," she muttered to herself, echoing the words she'd just read. *All includes me*, she thought. *I should do this. Cecilia's letter said, "God is the answer to everything," so what could it hurt?*

Her hand shook as she turned off the car. Her legs wobbled as she walked across the parking lot. She thought about her appearance. She hadn't worn makeup that day, and her sweater was a little wrinkled. She didn't have a Bible either. Her heart pounded in her chest, but she walked up the stairs anyway.

She reached for the door, her fingers brushing the red paint. It swung open before she could knock. There stood a man with kind eyes and laugh lines around his mouth. Stephanie guessed he was a pastor, although he wore no robe, just jeans and a plaid button-down shirt.

"H—Hi," she stammered. "I'm sorry. I wasn't sure if—"

The man spoke before she could finish. "Welcome home," he said.

Something in her chest cracked open. Her eyes welled up instantly, but she didn't cry.

"Oh, thank you," she said with a relieved exhale.

She stepped inside and looked around. The chapel was warm and unpretentious. Rows of simple chairs. A stage with a guitar on a stand and a few other instruments. No statues. No incense. No gilded gold on relics. Just a simple wooden cross and a few vases of wildflowers.

Stephanie took a seat near the back. The chapel smelled faintly of brewed coffee and freshly baked muffins. A child giggled somewhere near the front. The sunlight filtered through the unadorned glass windows, casting golden squares onto the floor.

The worship began with contemporary acoustic music that she had never heard before. People sang—not with showmanship but with sincerity. The lyrics were about grace and mercy, about being damaged yet welcome at the table.

She didn't sing. She didn't know the words. She just sat there, her hands folded in her lap, letting the songs wash over her like warm rain.

Then the man at the door, Pastor Rob, took to the podium and introduced himself.

His words were gentle but sure. He didn't raise his voice, and he didn't preach down to anyone. He talked about grief. About how pain doesn't mean God is absent. About how loss doesn't mean love was wasted. About how God meets us in the dark—right in the messy middle of our most difficult times.

Pastor Rob told a story about a cracked vase a woman had thrown away. She thought the vase had become worthless, but what she failed to see was that the cracks let the light through. "God doesn't discard the broken," the pastor said. "He uses them to shine."

Stephanie felt like every word of Pastor Rob's sermon was meant for her—that he'd spoken about her own life, her own cracked heart. He had stirred something inside of her, something hopeful.

She stayed after the service, sitting alone in her chair. Pastor Rob came over, and Stephanie introduced herself. She didn't tell him her whole story—she just said there had been deaths in the family, relatives she'd loved very much, and that she was trying to understand where God had gone.

Pastor Rob didn't offer clichés. He didn't try to fix her or guilt her for her wavering faith. He just nodded and said, "I'm glad you're here. Come back anytime."

The next week, she returned to the Sunday morning service. And she did the same the week after. And each time she went, by the end of the service, she felt better than when she'd entered.

She didn't go every week. Some days the grief was still too sharp. But she kept returning often, and she started bringing her family with her.

"Mom, they have puppets!" Gabriella cried out on her second visit to the children's room where volunteers played music and acted out Bible stories with felt characters. Jonathan liked the doughnuts after the service. Even Matthew, hesitant at first, appreciated the way nobody tried to pressure or convert him. Everyone there was just kind, present, and open.

Almost overnight, Sunday services became the highlight of Stephanie's week. She found herself counting down the days to the next Sunday. God's Word was reaching something deep within her, and each new insight felt like a personal revelation.

She immersed herself in the Bible, into this new congregation that was starting to feel more like a family. The people there remembered her, Matthew, and the children, and they always greeted them with warmth and friendly conversations.

One Sunday after the service, an older woman named June leaned over and said, "You have such a vibrant spirit, dear, and your family is beautiful. It's so nice to see you here."

Stephanie didn't know what to say. She just nodded and smiled, and later in the car she cried happy tears the whole way home.

She joined a Bible study group and then a women's group. She was shy at first and then became more open. The women were vulnerable and authentic. They didn't pretend to have all the answers. They talked about miscarriages, divorces, and children they couldn't reach. They talked about God like He was a friend, not a judge. Stephanie never knew church could be like this.

One woman, her eyes red, shared, "I used to think God was punishing me." Stephanie's breath caught, and she nodded in understanding. She knew that feeling. It had lived inside her for a long, long time, and she'd often wondered if she'd been alone in her feelings of abandonment.

Not long after Stephanie began going to the women's group, she signed up to help with the Saturday food pantry. She packed canned beans and boxes of cereal alongside a woman named Trina whose sweatshirt said, "Grace Wins." They didn't talk much. They just worked. But when Trina handed a box of cereal to this young mother with tired eyes, Stephanie felt something coming alive in her chest. A warmth. A purpose. She hadn't felt this useful in a long time.

Stephanie's journal entries began to change. They weren't just about rage and sorrow now—they were becoming reflections full of questions and hope. Sometimes she even smiled when she reread them. Little by little, the remaining bitterness inside her was beginning to thaw.

She began thinking that maybe faith isn't about feeling good, that maybe it's about refusing to let it go—even when you're furious, even when everything hurts. Gradually, Stephanie came to realize that God had never given up on her. He was the One who gave her strength, who held her up even now.

Stephanie began seeing a therapist. Slowly and cautiously she brought up her dreams, her guilt about having the charmed childhood that her brother didn't have, her confusion over how deeply she'd loved someone she'd only just met. She talked about the domino effect this all had on the ones around her, including how it had almost destroyed her relationship with her mother.

"I keep thinking I should've known," she began in one of her therapy sessions, "that something bad was coming. That I should have pushed Carmine harder to come north."

The therapist tilted her head. "Would it have changed anything?"

Stephanie hesitated. "No. But maybe I wouldn't feel so guilty."

Silence. Then softly the therapist replied, "Guilt is love that doesn't know where to go."

"With my mother gone, too, I don't know how to carry this," Stephanie said. "The world just keeps moving."

"You carry it in pieces," the therapist said, "a little at a time. You build a new life around the absence."

That night Stephanie dreamed of her brother standing outside the barbershop he never got to open. He was beaming, happy. He had hair clippers in one hand, coffee in the other.

"You're doing good, Sis," he said. "Keep going." He turned and pointed at the barbershop door—painted red, just like the chapel. "Go back," he said. "You'll find it there."

She awoke with tears on her cheeks. She reached for her Bible and opened it to a random page. Her eyes landed on Isaiah 43:2: "When you go through deep waters, I will be with you." She read it again. And again. It felt like Carmine's voice in the dream. Like Cecilia's letters. Like the red door.

She wrote the verse in her journal, underlined it twice, cut it out carefully with scissors, and taped it to her bathroom mirror. "He will be with me," she said to her reflection, believing in the words, believing in God's love.

∞ ∞ ∞

Two years after Stephanie first started going to Grace Fellowship, on a Sunday morning after the service, Pastor Rob approached her. "Stephanie, can I steal you for a moment?" He gestured toward a quiet corner of the sanctuary, away from the crowd.

"Of course, Pastor Rob." She followed him with curiosity.

"I've been praying about Easter Sunday," he continued. "It's such a powerful time, one of resurrection, renewal, and hope. And I keep coming back to you."

"Me?" she asked.

"Yes. About you and your journey. It's one of the most honest, courageous transformations I've witnessed. I think it's time to share it. Would you consider giving your testimony on Easter?"

Stephanie hesitated. "I . . . don't know. I mean . . . I wouldn't even know where to start."

Pastor Rob's face lit up. "Start with your heart. The rest will follow. You don't have to be polished—you just have to be authentic and true. And I'll be here to help you shape your speech if you like."

"That's such a big thing," Stephanie replied. "An honor, but . . . but such a big thing."

Pastor Rob's eyes sparkled. "You've lived through the valley. Now let others see how God walked with you through it."

Stephanie hesitated again, but with Pastor Rob's counsel and warm encouragement, she agreed.

She worked on her testimony for two weeks—going back through her journals, rereading Carmine's old texts and emails, revisiting Cecilia's letters, remembering her mom's burial, reliving the Brooklyn trip. Writing for an audience was hard at first, but then the words started pouring out of her. On the Saturday before Easter, Matthew helped her clean up her testimony and listened as she practiced reading it out loud.

On Easter Sunday, before leaving the house, Stephanie fastened Cecilia's silver locket around her neck and slipped a sapphire ring of Angelina's onto her finger. She paused at her bedroom mirror, staring at her own reflection. The deep blue ring glinted in the morning light. It was Angelina's favorite color and her birthstone. Stephanie closed her eyes and whispered to both of them, "Be with me."

After his sermon that morning, with the light streaming through the windows, Pastor Rob introduced Stephanie and invited her up to the front of the chapel. A wave of nerves shot through her as she walked down the aisle to the podium. Her heart pounded, not from fear but from the weight of what she was about to share.

She took a big breath to give herself a moment to adjust to the many eyes upon her. She cleared her throat.

Her voice trembled at first. "I used to think grief was a wall," she said. "But it's a doorway—one you walk through slowly with scraped knees and open hands." She saw heads nodding in the audience. Then the words started coming comfortably, and she looked out into the faces of the people she had grown to love and who now loved her.

Feeling more grounded, she kept going. When she was finished, tears glistened on the cheeks of almost everyone in the room. Something deep within her eased, like a small catharsis.

After the service, a young woman approached her. She'd lost her sister two years earlier in a motorcycle accident.

"I thought I was alone," the woman said breathlessly.

"You're not," Stephanie said, pulling her into a hug. "None of us are." The woman nodded, tears streaking her cheeks. After the embrace, Stephanie held the woman's hand a moment, as if anchoring them both to something sacred.

It seemed as if spring came early that year. The trees bloomed more brightly. The sky felt softer, like the whole world was leaning toward renewal. Stephanie walked beneath the cherry blossoms one morning and thought, *Even the trees know how to begin again.* She remembered how much Angelina had loved springtime.

The house felt warmer. Laughter came more easily. Stephanie spent more time in the garden with her kids and husband. She smiled more and felt lighter. And in that garden, with dirt under her fingernails and her children beside her, Stephanie often glanced at Matthew and felt something deep and steady—not just love, but peace.

One Sunday afternoon before the service, she walked up to the chapel and touched the red door again.

"Thank you," she said reverently, gratefully.

The grief remained—it always would. But so did grace. So did love. So did hope.

And somewhere in the quiet of her soul, something whispered back.

Welcome home.

Stephanie's Testimony (Easter Sunday, 2011)

Happy Resurrection Sunday, everyone. Before I begin, I want to express how deeply honored I am that Pastor Rob invited me to give my testimony today. It's a privilege that humbles me.

My name is Stephanie DeRosa, and I live here in Point Pleasant with my husband, Matthew, and our children, Jonathan and Gabriella, the lights of my life.

Most of you here at Grace Fellowship know me by now. My family and I began attending about two years ago. When I was baptized last year, I shared a public, emotional proclamation, but I didn't share my story.

I don't offer it easily. But today, I'm ready. I've come to care deeply for this church family, and I trust you. You are all beautiful—each of you—in your own unique way.

I have learned throughout my life that everyone has a story, and this is mine. I used to think grief was a wall, but it's a doorway—one you walk through slowly with scraped knees and open hands. Let me tell you about how I got here, living in light with the Lord.

I was born in Brooklyn, New York, the only child of two wonderful parents. I grew up in an extended, loving, protective, loud, fun, and very typical Italian-American family. My early life was happy and safe. I was privileged and, truthfully, a bit of a spoiled brat.

I attended a Catholic grammar school, and I resented it for years afterward. Only recently have I come to see it differently because it was there that my love for Christ began. It was there that I accepted Him as my Savior.

As a child, I joined the Girl Scouts, took extensive dance classes, and always believed—perhaps naively—that greatness lay ahead for me. But even back then, something felt off. I remember that feeling as early as age eight, and I remember wondering why I was an only child. I had a gut instinct telling me I was different from the rest of the family. And every time I asked about it, I was told I was being silly. That my doubts weren't true.

Except for that, my childhood was lovely, as I've said. But my perfect world came crashing down when I was just fourteen years old. That was when my father was diagnosed with pancreatic cancer. I was truly daddy's little girl, and I was terrified.

He fought the illness bravely for nearly a year. I remember yelling at the priest who came to give him his Last Rites, telling him to leave. God had always given me everything I'd asked for, and He was not going to take my daddy.

It still feels like yesterday. When my father first became ill, he promised he'd be there for my sweet sixteen, my prom, and to walk me down the aisle. So I believed him. And the funny thing is . . . he was. He did all that and more, despite his passing. I've felt him with me, always. Right here beside me.

I sure gave my mom a hard time after that. My teenage years were filled with anger, rebellion, and hopelessness. Because of me, Mom had countless sleepless nights. I broke curfew, lied about where I'd been, and snuck out to go into Manhattan. And I gave her more than a few gray hairs in the process.

But as I grew older, I matured. Mom and I became very close. I cherished her and cared for her in every way I could. I went to work straight out of high school to help with the bills and ensure we both had everything we needed. We leaned on each other because, truthfully, there was nowhere else to lean.

Yet still, I always felt like something wasn't quite right.

Eventually, I landed an amazing job in Manhattan, despite not having a college degree. I was lucky.

After a few years of working, I met a great guy. We married and had two beautiful children. One of them has special needs and is wonderfully different. And that difference is a gift—not a burden. My son is perfectly himself, just like the Lord made him.

Right after I turned forty, we bought a beautiful house here in Point Pleasant. I was as pleased as could be. I truly thought life couldn't get any better.

Our new house even had a small apartment attached, and we moved my mother in with us. What a blessing it was to have her—my children's grandmother—living right there with us.

But as always, something didn't feel quite right. That sensation had never gone away. In fact, it had only grown stronger over the years.

Just after we moved in, I was unpacking some boxes when the phone rang. On the other end of the line, a woman asked to speak to Stephanie Pellegrino. I thought that was strange. Why was someone asking for me by my maiden name? The woman went on to tell me she was a private investigator and genealogist. Then she asked, "Were you ever told you were adopted?"

And there it was. That was the thing that had been "off" in my life—part of it anyway.

She went on to tell me I had a full biological brother who'd been searching for me for four years—ever since he'd learned about me. His name was Carmine. He lived in Florida.

That evening, I confronted my mom. She turned white as a sheet, and we fought. Finally, she confessed to what I'd known in my heart all along: I was adopted. Mom said she kept it a secret from me because she was always afraid of losing me.

I was devastated. Confused. Hurt. Betrayed by the very people I loved.

And yet, to me, God was still good. I now had a sibling—a brother. Who could ask for more? I'd always wanted a brother or sister, and I was thrilled. Carmine and I spoke on the phone every day, all day, getting to know each other.

We were just two weeks shy of a year apart. I was told that my biological mother, having regretted her decision to give me up, had sought to "replace" me immediately. She wasn't married when I was born—that's why her family made her give me up—but by the time Carmine came along, she had wed our biological father.

And when my brother showed me a picture of her, I saw that I look just like her. At long last I actually looked like someone. Not resembling anyone in my family had always bothered me, but now, when I saw my birth mom's pictures, it was like looking into a mirror.

Sadly, my birth mom had passed away long before any of this came to light. She'd died young of cancer, at age thirty-five. I was told she had a very rough life, one filled with addiction and instability.

But the craziest part of all this—the part that still sends a shiver up my spine—is that my brother and I were raised in the same Brooklyn neighborhood, Bensonhurst. We knew the same people. We went to the same high school. We were, most likely, shoulder-to-shoulder at various points, yet we never knew the truth.

My brother and I started visiting each other, going back and forth between New Jersey and Florida. And every time I saw him, it was like time folded in on itself, like we were two puzzle pieces that fit perfectly.

God brought my brother and me together, just like that. And it's one of the deepest connections I've ever known. But we didn't have much time together. He died in a car accident—going 90 miles an hour into a palm tree.

I had four months with my brother in my life. Just three in-person visits.

You see, my brother spent his life trying to close his wounds and hide his scars because his upbringing was tough—nothing like mine. I always felt guilty about that, yet I couldn't be his savior. As much as he wanted me to be, as much as he yearned for it, I couldn't save him.

After that, God and I weren't on the best of terms. But deep down, I still loved Jesus. I didn't understand Him, but I still loved Him underneath my anger and heartbreak.

I must believe that Carmine loves the Lord now, in Heaven.

Through all the grief—emotional and physical—I still had faith. I missed Carmine—miss him still—but I had faith.

And I still had Matthew. He's not just my husband. He's my friend. My steady place. He's an extraordinary father, and I am forever grateful.

We've weathered storms that could have torn us apart, but somehow we stayed, not out of obligation but out of devotion. Out of love that's been tested—and refined.

My mom left this life not long ago. A massive heart attack put her in the ICU. I stayed by her bedside in the hospital for eleven days straight. She begged me for forgiveness—but I had already given it.

Forgiveness is the most beautiful gift you can give—to yourself or to someone else. I pray that she forgives me too. I put her through so much.

While holding Mom's hand and stroking her gently, I witnessed her passing into Paradise. I watched as her eyes opened into the radiance and glory of God, and it was one of the most beautiful experiences I've ever witnessed. Thinking of it still takes my breath away.

I told her she could go dance with my dad again . . . kiss Carmine for me . . . and thank my biological mom for the gift of life. I miss my mother terribly, but God is with us through all the happiness and tragedy we encounter in life—some of it big, some of it small.

Jesus Christ has held me up through my hardest times. Every time my knees buckled, He gave me the strength of a bull—strength I never dreamed I could have. There's no other way to explain it. That strength is one of the many ways He reveals Himself to me. I love Him and believe all praise belongs to Him.

Pastor Rob gave me some pointers on preparing my testimony for today. One of them was to share how Jesus shows His love to me.

Well, Jesus gives me the warmth of a father's embrace—wrapped around me daily. I truly feel it. I see it in my children's eyes, in their smiles. I see the light of His love in the comings and goings of everyday life, even in this crazy world.

His love gives me the tenacity to move forward. It gives me encouragement and hope. I have a beautiful, personal relationship with Him. I know I'm far, far from perfect. But only through Him do I have the strength to be the woman, the mother, the friend, and the person I strive to be. I am, and I will always be, a work in progress. And I'm savoring every minute of my walk with the Lord.

I'm surrounded by wonderful, supportive people. I see love in each and every one of you, all the time, and I thank you for that. I'm sure you don't even realize it, but many of you are my mentors, my inspiration.

Thank you for your encouragement and prayers, for your hugs, your smiles. Thank you—from the bottom of my heart—for being kind and welcoming to my family.

And then there's salvation. Because He died on the cross for me, I have salvation. That's the bottom line. My sins—can you believe it?—my sins are forgiven. Now I move forward, excited about what's ahead.

Pastor Rob, you said to share what He has done for me. I can only sum it up by saying, every single thing.

I'm on the path I've always wanted to be on—I'm just finally figuring out how to walk it. I am standing. Hallelujah!

Life is good now. But there will always be bumps in the road—ones we can all get through with Jesus by our side.

I want to live by His example every day, through all my trials and tribulations.

To me, that's the only thing that truly matters. Everything else falls into place from there.

For the people I encounter daily—my family and friends—I want them to see and know Jesus through me.

I sing in church now, something I never did before. Now I lift Him up with my voice. Jesus makes me smile. He makes me rejoice.

I could have cut this testimony into a three-second sentence. One that reflects my ultimate revelation, and it is true for all of us: HE. LOVES. ME.

I end with a verse from the Gospel of John 16:33, which truly speaks to me. I hope it speaks to you too. "I have told you all this so that you may have peace in me. Here on earth you will have many trials and sorrows. But take heart, because I have overcome the world."

Thank you.

Author's Note

I used to believe silence was unbreakable, that the things we never spoke about would remain buried forever. I used to believe some questions had no answers and that some absences were simply part of who we were meant to be. But I know better now.

The silence that once defined me is no longer empty. It has a name, a face, and a story. It is my brother. For too short a time, he was no longer just a shadow on the edge of my life but a living part of it. Our laughter, our late-night phone calls, and our shared memories stitched together a bond I never imagined possible. That bond did not end the day he left this earth.

I still carry my brother with me. I carry him when I talk to my children about the uncle they came to know, even if just for a brief season. I carry him when I walk into the places we dreamed of visiting together, praying that he sees them through my eyes. I carry him in the quiet of the night when grief presses close, and in the mornings when faith nudges me forward.

The silence that shaped my life is now filled with memory, with love, with the knowledge that even what we lose can still leave a mark that endures.

My brother taught me that family is not measured in years but in connection. That even what is hidden can be found, and even what is lost can still be cherished. His story did not end with tragedy—it continues in the way I live, in the way I forgive, in the way I believe. When I think of him, I don't just remember how his story ended. I remember that for a moment—brief but real—we found each other. And that will always matter.

I used to think silence was stronger than I was, but I have learned that silence is never the final word. Love is. And what the heart carries—love, memory, redemption—remains. Always.

Acknowledgments

Thank you to:

J&G. You give my life meaning and purpose. You both inspire me in a million different ways. I will love you until my last breath and beyond.

Mom and Dad for giving me the very best childhood, full of unconditional love and joy. Nothing other than that matters now. I love and miss you both so much.

My birth mother for giving me the gift of life. I pray you have found peace and self-forgiveness.

My brother for finding me and bringing the truth to light. I miss you terribly, and I love you.

My husband, for pushing me to get out of my own way and finally put pen to paper. I couldn't have done this without you. You gave me the courage to see this long-delayed story come to life, and I love you.

My extended family. I am so sorry for the weight that was put on all of you. I'm eternally grateful for all the love you've always given to me as if I were your blood. It was never even a question. Through all our craziness and amazing memories, I love you all.

The beautiful family on 19th Avenue. You embraced me instantly, and I will always adore every one of you. I am so very grateful that you are in my life, and I am humbled by the love and care that you show me to this day. I cannot imagine my life without all of you in it. You will always be my family and in my heart. Yes, all of you.

Erika DeSimone for your knowledge, professionalism, and dedication. I couldn't have asked for a better editor and writing coach.

God, for my messy, complicated, beautiful life and all the strength You give me. All the glory belongs to You.

About the Author

Susan Appel writes from the heart, drawing on her own family history of loss, resilience, and redemption. *What the Heart Carries: One Secret, Two Lives* is inspired by true events that shaped Susan's understanding of love, faith, and the bonds that endure even through tragedy. Through vivid storytelling and heartfelt honesty, her work explores themes of identity, grief, and the unbreakable ties of family.

Susan cherishes quiet moments and laughter-filled days with her husband and two children. She finds joy in simple traditions, lasting friendships, and the spiritual journey that continues to guide her steps. *What the Heart Carries* is her first novel, crafted with the hope of reaching others who have faced grief, family secrets, or the pursuit of hidden truths. She believes deeply in the power of words to heal, to connect, and to remind us that even in life's darkest seasons, hope can be found.

www.ingramcontent.com/pod-product-compliance
Lightning Source LLC
LaVergne TN
LVHW010612100826
845148LV00014B/2928

* 9 7 8 1 6 3 2 9 6 9 6 7 5 *